The
Farringford Journal of
EMILY TENNYSON
1853 - 1864

ISLE OF WIGHT COUNTY PRESS

The
Farringford Journal
of
Emily Tennyson

1853 - 1864

Edited by

RICHARD J. HUTCHINGS
and
BRIAN HINTON

First published 1986

ISBN 0 9510379 1 9

Printed and published by
The Isle of Wight County Press
29 High Street - Newport
Isle of Wight - PO30 1ST

Contents

Illustrations

Preface

Emily Tennyson began writing a journal in 1850, the year she married Alfred Tennyson the poet, and continued during their idyllically happy marriage on the Isle of Wight and at Aldworth in West Sussex. This book contains a record of the first ten years of their marriage at Farringford. The only complete version of the journal, 1850 to 1874, was published in 1981 by the University Press of Virginia and edited by James O. Hoge. It is a copy of the journal written in Emily's own hand and now in the Tennyson Research Centre, Lincoln. However, even that had to be edited and rewritten by Emily when she was helping her son, Hallam, to prepare the *Memoir* (in two volumes) of his father in the 1890s. The original copy of the journal was destroyed. What we are left with is an account of daily events in the Tennyson household – the poet's activities, visits, visitors, his literary works and reading. Moreover, we have an intimate glimpse of family life at Farringford while Tennyson was writing some of his greatest works.

Although Professor Hoge's edition of Lady Tennyson's Journal has been of immense value to us in the especially difficult task of interpreting Emily Tennyson's handwriting, we have nonetheless relied totally on the original journal in Emily's hand for our final interpretation. Editorial notes, comments and precis are shown in square brackets in the text, and where Emily's manuscript is illegible we have completed the sense to the best of our ability. The Epilogue is a summation of the Tennysons' years at Farringford, placing their lives in perspective with the Victorian age.

As we were limited in the number of pages for this edition, it was necessary to work to a strict editorial policy, rather than selecting passages at random from the journal. The introductory chapter describes briefly the family backgrounds of the Tennysons and the Sellwoods, the long engagement of Alfred to Emily, their marriage and move to the Island, as well as discussing Tennyson's work written after 1853. We have selected the first ten years of their marriage at Farringford because during that period the Tennysons spent more time at home when the children were young, than in the latter ten years, 1865 to 1874, when the children were sent to boarding schools and the parents travelled extensively. Even so, during the early period at Farringford, the Tennysons (more often the poet on his own) contrived to find reasons for leaving the Island each year. But in 1874, Emily Tennyson was stricken down with a serious illness and was forced to stop writing her Journal. Hallam, their eldest boy, was recalled from Cambridge University to take over Emily's task as secretary and amanuensis to the poet.

By 1874 the Tennysons had attracted to Farringford an intimate circle of friends – the Simeons of Swainston, the Camerons of Dimbola, the Watts and Prinseps of The Briary, the Wards of Weston Manor and the Granville Bradleys of Heathfield. There were also other dear friends and neighbours such as the Hamonds of Afton Manor, the Croziers of Yarmouth and the Thackeray daughters, Anne and Harriet Marian (Minny).

W. G. Ward's son, Wilfrid, described Freshwater in its Victorian heyday as seething with intellectual life. If Tennyson was revered as 'King Alfred' in the social hierarchy of Freshwater, then Mrs. Cameron, the eccentric photographer, was 'Prime Minister' in so far as she stage-managed everyone, friends, neighbours and visitors who were rash enough to stray within her territory. Anne Thackeray, the novelist's eldest daughter, said that everybody in Freshwater was 'either a genius, or a poet, or a painter or peculiar in some way; poor Miss Stephen says "Is there *nobody* commonplace?"' Mrs. Cameron's 'premiership' lasted from 1860 to 1875, and during that period her never-ending quest was to capture Beauty with her camera. She was no respecter of persons, whether of genius or nobility, and her manner could be overbearing, domineering and interfering. But her one saving grace was her smiling benevolence and her sometimes immoderate generosity which could be exceedingly embarrassing to the recipient. Thomas Carlyle once remarked on receiving a prayer-book as a Christmas gift that 'either the Devil or Mrs. Cameron must have sent me this!' Wilfrid Ward recalled that when Tennyson was writing the *Idylls of the King,* Mrs. Cameron brought him to his father's manor house while she was photographing representatives for the characters, and called out directly she saw Cardinal Vaughan (to whom she was a perfect stranger): 'Alfred I have found Sir Launcelot'. Tennyson's reply was: 'I want a face well worn with evil passion'.

Anecdotes about the Camerons are legion, and the manner of their departure from Freshwater in 1875, illustrates their eccentricities admirably. Charles Hay Cameron, Julia's husband, frequently wore a blue dressing gown and during the twelve years of his residence at Dimbola he never wandered beyond its boundaries, but suddenly one day he asked to borrow his son's coat and went down to Freshwater Bay, and seeing the Channel before his eyes he yearned to return to his coffee estates in Ceylon. Back at the house he told Julia of his decision and immediately she organised everything for their departure – taking their coffins with them. The last sight of them on board ship was of Julia Cameron presenting porters with large photographs of Sir Henry Taylor, her favourite poet, and the Madonna 'in default of small change', as Virginia Woolf put it. Mrs. Cameron died in Ceylon in 1879 and her husband a year later. *Annals of My Glass House* remains as Mrs. Cameron's own record of her photographic venture which led to international fame.

In 1862 G. F. Watts painted several portraits of the Tennyson family, and he and the Prinseps were guests of Mrs. Cameron in Terrace Lane, Freshwater Bay. Ten years later he built The Briary, near Farringford, for his patrons, the Prinseps (Mrs. Sarah Prinsep and Mrs. Cameron were two of the famous Pattle sisters), but he spent much of his time at their Kensington home, Little Holland House, till it was demolished in 1875. A year later he built a new Little Holland House after wintering in the Island with the Prinseps. He was a frequent visitor to Freshwater and became one of Tennyson's closest friends. His marriage to Ellen Terry in 1864 was a disaster and the following year they separated and ultimately divorced. His second marriage was to Mary Fraser Tytler in 1886. The poet at first had thought of Watts as too much the aesthete – for he lived isolated in his 'Palace of Art' and the real world seemed of little consequence to him. But later the poet came to admire the man and the artist –

> As when a painter posing on a face,
> Divinely, thro' all hindrance, finds the man
> Behind it and so paints him that his face,
> The shape and colour of a mind and life,
> Lives for his children, ever at its best.

Tennyson's 'Prince of Courtesy', Sir John Simeon, was a genial, fox-hunting Catholic squire with a penchant for the company of poets. They had met earlier, but their friendship flourished in 1854 when Sir John induced him to write *Maud* based on four lines of previously published verse. Their friendship remained very close even though the poet was a liberal-minded Protestant and strongly opposed blood sports. He felt Sir John's loss grievously in 1870.

Three years elapsed before he transferred his friendship to another Catholic, W. G. Ward (known as 'Ideal' Ward), a scholar and philosopher whom he considered to be the 'most generous of all ultramontanes'. They probably met for the first time in 1862 (see Emily Tennyson's Journal, 26 October) even though Ward had inherited from his uncle in

1849 Island estates at Weston Manor and Northwood Park. Tennyson once said of him: 'If I had Ward's blind faith, I should always be happy'. But at the same time the poet was on equally intimate terms with the Christian Socialists, F. D. Maurice and Charles Kingsley.

In particular in 1854 he renewed his friendship with Granville Bradley, the future Dean of Westminster. He was then Headmaster of Marlborough and later Master of University College, Oxford. The two men would roam the Island sometimes from midday till ten at night, talking almost ceaselessly, 'poetizing, botanizing, geologizing'. Bradley was many years younger than Tennyson and outlived him by eleven years, seeing in the new century and the coronation of King Edward VII.

Anne Thackeray and her sister 'Minny', were particular favourites of the Tennysons and the Camerons, and after their father's death in December 1863, they were virtually adopted by them. They usually stayed at The Porch near Dimbola, Freshwater Bay. Anne was a distinguished author in her own right and had recently published her first novel, *The Story of Elizabeth*. Towards the end of his life, Tennyson asked Anne to accept a commission from *Harper's* to write a monograph of himself; he could think of no one better fitted for the work. Anne married Richmond Ritchie, her second cousin, a high-ranking civil servant. At The Porch she wrote *From an Island* (1872) and *From the Porch* (1913), and during World War One she made the cottage her home. Anne Thackeray's daughter, Hester Fuller, also wrote memoirs of those days in *Three Freshwater Friends*, and, with Violet Hammersley, published *Thackeray's Daughters* in 1951.

'Minny' Thackeray married Leslie Stephen, the distinguished scholar and editor of the *Dictionary of National Biography*. They had one daughter, Paula. 'Minny' died in November 1875, and her widower married Julia Duckworth, the daughter of Maria Jackson, another of the Pattle sisters. They had four very talented children, Vanessa Bell, Thoby, Virginia Woolf and Adrian. Virginia wrote the satirical drama, *Freshwater*, for the stage. It explored lightheartedly the relationships between Tennyson, the Camerons, G. F. Watts and Ellen Terry, his wife, and a fictitious gentleman named John Craig, her paramour.

The real value of Emily Tennyson's Journal is not so much literary as biographical and historical. It is an essential source of reference for any Life of the poet, and its publication in this country is long overdue. We hope it will add immensely to the Tennysonian heritage of the Isle of Wight, for here, encapsulated for all time, is a record of the Vectensian Athens of the nineteenth century, where the poet spent the mature half of his life and wrote, arguably, some of his greatest works – *Maud,*

Enoch Arden and *Idylls of the King*. It is regrettable that so few memorabilia of the poet's stay remain in the Island. We hope that by publishing a decade of Emily Tennyson's Farringford Journal we may compensate for the discrepancy, and that it will stimulate interest in the poet's associations with the Island and in the work he did here.

Acknowledgements

Acknowledgements to the Lincolnshire County Council, owners of the manuscript copy of Emily Lady Tennyson's Journal at the Tennyson Research Centre, Lincoln, for permission to publish selections from it, and for the illustrations from the Tennyson Research Centre Collection, Lincoln, by courtesy of Lord Tennyson and Lincolnshire Library Service; to Mr. R. M. Lyle, Assistant Director of Recreational Services in charge of Libraries and Archives, and to Miss S. Gates and the staff of the public library, Free School Lane, Lincoln for research facilities; to the Rector and Visitors of the University Press of Virginia, U.S.A., copyright holders of the published version of Lady Tennyson's Journal in America, edited and introduced by James O. Hoge; to Mr. L. J. Mitchell, Director of Cultural Services for the Isle of Wight, for valuable assistance; in particular our indebtedness to the former Isle of Wight Tourist Board and its Director, Mr. Ewen Brenchley, for encouraging and supporting our researches in Lincoln. Finally we are particularly grateful to Mr. Laurence Elvin, F.S.A., F.R.Hist.S., F.R.S.A., of the Tennyson Society for reading through the editorial sections of the manuscript and for giving us encouragement in this enterprise.

The Long Engagement – Introductory

The turning-point in Alfred Tennyson's career came in 1850 at the age of forty-one. He was at last happily married and his poem *In Memoriam,* dedicated to his dear friend, Arthur Henry Hallam, who died in 1833, was a phenomenal success running into three editions in the first year. On its merits he was appointed Poet Laureate on the recommendation of Prince Albert, the Queen's consort. With the money received from his poems, pension, annuities and investments, he was in 1856 able to buy Farringford House at Freshwater on the Isle of Wight where he lived for forty years. For one who was impecunious during the first forty years and suffered considerable emotional stress, this fortuitous turn of events, this fame, prosperity and peace of mind, was profoundly welcome. But he never forgot his early years, which began at Somersby Rectory in Lincolnshire on 6 August 1809.

Alfred Tennyson was the fourth son in a family of twelve children – the first-born, George, died in infancy. He and his two elder brothers Frederick and Charles, were all to become poets of considerable talent. Their father, the Reverend George Clayton Tennyson, was the incumbent of the adjoining parishes of Somersby and Bag Enderby, but he was a morose, moody and sometimes violent man, the violence brought on by excessive drinking. Although educated away from home, the boys obtained from him a sound classical schooling and fanatical interest in poetry. Alfred inherited his father's moodiness and melancholy which was not helped by the family's lack of money.

His wife, christened Emily Sarah Sellwood, was born 9 July 1813, the eldest daughter of Henry Sellwood a Horncastle solicitor and the son of a landed Berkshire family whose fortunes declined in the previous generation. Emily and her two sisters, Anne and Louisa, were cousins of the Cracrofts of Harrington Hall, situated in the wolds a few miles from Somersby Rectory. Their mother was one of the seven sisters of Arctic explorer, Sir John Franklin.

Alfred met Emily in Holywell Wood when she was with Arthur Hallam. She was dressed in a light blue costume, the sight of which provoked him to ask her, 'Are you a Dryad or an Oread, wandering here?' and she instantly fell in love with him. The Tennysons and the Sellwoods first met in 1830. However, Alfred's first love was Rosa Baring, whose stepfather Admiral Arthur Eden rented Harrington Hall (owned by the Cracrofts). Rosa was the youngest of three daughters, the other two being Fanny and Georgina. But where Emily Sellwood was an invalid from birth, was wanly pretty, unworldly and deeply religious, Rosa was a beautiful, vivacious coquette from a wealthy, socially well-connected, aristocratic family. Alfred was infatuated with her, but soon realised that there was no depth to her feeling for him. In any case there was such a vast disparity in the fortunes of Rosa's family and his own that marriage was out of the question.

Emily's feeling for Alfred Tennyson were reciprocated when together they attended the wedding of Charles Tennyson and Emily's sister, Louisa, in 1836. But Alfred never really forgot Rosa and her character is portrayed in a number of his early female vignettes written in the 1830s, such as 'The Day-Dream', 'To Rosa' and 'The Gardener's Daughter', as well as in a later poem 'Roses on the Terrace'. *Maud* is also said to be based on the character of Rosa Baring.

Alfred and Emily became engaged, but their marriage was delayed because of the poet's lack of prospects, his loss of Christian faith and periodical mental breakdowns. At times it seemed they would never marry as the years dragged by. But when she read Alfred's 'Elegies' to the memory of Arthur Henry Hallam, later to be renamed *In Memoriam A.H.H.*, she felt there was no longer any question about Alfred's Christian faith, although earlier he himself had expressed reservations to Emily in the 'Elegies' when he argued that perhaps it is preferable to doubt sometimes rather than be dogmatic in one's belief.

Doubts or not, Alfred and Emily were married at Shiplake on 13 June 1850. Tennyson first got to know about Farringford when he was staying with the Rev. James White at Bonchurch, and having gone over there, 'he found it looking wretched with wet leaves trampled into the lawn'. It was enclosed in trees and shrubberies, and the walls were covered with creepers, so that the interior was very gloomy and dark. But he was pleased with it and he wrote to Emily saying that they must visit it together soon.

The Georgian house was built in 1806, but was enlarged four years later, so that when the Tennysons arrived there were fifteen rooms. In appearance it reminded them of Somersby Rectory in Lincolnshire. They fell in love at first sight with the secluded house with its Gothic-style windows and castellated walls – that nestled so romantically among the ancient trees and undulating meadows. To the south the magnificently swelling slopes of green High Down (now Tennyson Down) were an open invitation to walk, an invitation the poet rarely refused on his daily rounds. To seaward the down fell away precipitously for hundreds of feet in a 'milky steep' of chalk cliffs, and its extremities were at the Needles and at Freshwater Gate, where the sound of the sea on the shingly beach was a 'broad-flung ship-wrecking roar'.

The early records of the estate go back to the fourteenth century, and the name of one witness, Walter de Ferringford, appears most frequently on the title deeds. The present home stands near the site of the original Prior's Manor, which then belonged to the Abbey of Lyra in Normandy. The farmland adjacent (part of the estate in Tennyson's day) was of nearly three hundred acres and included fields retaining their original names – Prior's Field, Maiden's Croft (dedicated to the Virgin Mary), the Clerk's Hill (where the clerk of the monastery lived), St. George (where the archers shot) and Abraham's Mead.

In 1853 the purchase price of the Farringford estate was £4,350, whereas three years later it had increased to £6,900, Tennyson was well able to turn down his publisher's advance of £1,000 because in that year he had earned £2,058 from his poetry. Ten thousand copies of *In Memoriam A.H.H.* had been sold in 1850. So that now in 1856, in addition to the amount earned by his poetry he was receiving also £100 for the laureateship, another £100 from his Aunt Russell, plus Emily's inheritance of £500 and the £200 Civil List pension. He was also receiving dividends from his railway investments, which made him one of the wealthiest poets this country had known.

Domestic reasons aside, the Tennysons retreated to West Wight from Chapel House, Twickenham to avoid the eternal round of socializing in London. The unremitting attentions of his City friends and acquaintances had begun to interfere with the progress of his work. The island's unique natural setting provided the right stimulus, isolation and topographical detail for such poems as the romantic monodrama, *Maud* (1855) and his most popular work, *Enoch Arden* (1864). Moreover, when eventually Emily and their sons, Hallam and Lionel, were happily ensconced at Farringford, he found what he had not previously experienced, a sense of domestic and financial security which bolstered his self-confidence so much he was able to begin work on the *Idylls of the King*.

Without a doubt, the *Idylls* written mainly at Farringford, did more to strengthen the ties of genuine friendship between the royal family and the laureate than any other of his poems. In one of Prince Albert's last letters from Buckingham Palace, written on 17 May 1860, which was accompanied by a copy of the *Idylls,* he asked the poet to autograph it, and added, 'They quite kindle the feeling with which the legends of King Arthur must have inspired the chivalry of old, whilst the graceful form in which they are presented blends those feelings with the softer tone of our own age . . .' *Idylls of the King* is, perhaps, the greatest 'laureate' work ever written in the English language, although it was never intended as such in its conception. The allegorical *Idylls* of the Farringford years were a derivative of the earlier Arthurian romantic lyrics, *The Lady of Shalott* (1832), *Sir Galahad, Sir Launcelot and Queen Guinevere, The Epic* and *Morte d'Arthur* (1842). These poems were written with the character of Arthur Henry Hallam in mind. Tennyson's first attempts to write the *Idylls* can be traced to the year 1857, when he printed, but did not publish *Enid and Nimuë: or The True and the False*. After the 1859 *Idylls* appeared, others followed in the 1862 edition dedicated to the late Prince Albert; then the 1872 edition, and to complete the twelve books, *Balin and Balan* in 1885. But Tennyson was not yet finished with King Arthur, because in 1889 he published *Merlin and the Gleam* in which the Gleam is represented as 'the higher poetic imagination'. Altogether the Arthurian legends preoccupied him nearly all his working life, but it was Emily's Farringford which created the right mental climate for the *Idylls*.

In time Tennyson built himself a summer-house on the northern edge of Maiden's Croft meadow where he could admire 'the afterglow on the trees in St. George's (the mediaeval-looking field beyond), and would talk about the stars'. Here he wrote *Enoch Arden*, and like the shipwrecked hero returning home after a long absence, he drew in 'down thro' all his blood . . . the dewy meadowy morning-breath of England . . .' Here too he wrote *The Holy Grail*, over which he had long vacillated, fearing that, in writing it, he might incur a charge of irreverence from the established Church.

William Thackeray, an old friend, once said of Tennyson that he considered him one of the wisest men he knew. The poet was a devoted family man, keen geologist, botanist and astronomer. Thomas Carlyle thought him 'one of the finest looking men in the world – a great shock of rough dusky dark hair; bright laughing hazel eyes; massive aquiline face, most massive yet most delicate; of sallow brown complexion, almost Indian looking; clothes cynically loose, free-and-easy, smokes infinite tobacco. His voice is musical, metallic, fit for loud laughter and piercing wail, and all that may lie between; speech and speculation free and plenteous; I do not meet in these late decades such company over a pipe!'

Sir Charles Tennyson in his biography of the poet records impressions of Emily by a Miss Southwell, governess-companion at Afton Manor, who clearly remembered that Emily always seemed to be seated in her drawing-room, writing letters, dressed 'in grey merino, with a long train, trimmed with velour or fur, and a piece of rich old lace, worn instead of a cap, drooping gracefully down over the train behind and coming to a point in front'. She dedicated her life to being her husband's secretary although she was frequently ill. Tennyson loathed writing letters, mainly for the reason that they were a distraction from his poetry writing. There were letters from royalty, friends and the general public; there were begging letters, letters from aspiring poets wanting criticism of their work, and of course the usual business correspondence. Emily tackled the task bravely, tactfully and uncomplainingly. She also attended to domestic affairs, the servants, the education of the boys and not least the welfare of her husband. Beneath her frail exterior was a will of iron and a strong sense of wifely duty, and in return she received from Alfred and her sons an effusion of love. They built her a hand-drawn carriage in which they trundled her about the grounds of Farringford and along the downs, a happy laughing band.

Margaret L. Wood's mother, a close friend of the Tennysons, recalls evenings in the Farringford drawing-room, how, when she first entered the room, Emily would rise from her couch and glide toward her with welcoming smile.

> She always wore a soft grey cashmere gown, and it was always made in the same simple fashion . . . Her silky auburn-brown hair, partly hidden by lace lappets, was untouched with grey, and her complexion kept its rose-leaf delicacy, just as her strong and cultivated intellect kept its alertness, to the last days of her life. No sooner were the greetings over than ten to one the door would open, and the Poet would come slowly, softly, silently into the room, dressed in an old-fashioned black tail-coat, and fixing my mother with his short-sighted gaze. One day, she being seated with her back to the cedar-green window, he approached her with such extreme deference, and so solemn a courtesy, as made her all amazed; until in a minute, with a flash of amusement, both discovered that he had mistaken her for – the Queen. Still more surely one or both of the long-haired, grey tunicked boys would appear, less silently; and away the children scampered to their endless play about the rambling house and grounds. But even the children's play was informed with the vital interest of the two houses: the story of King Arthur and the knights. The first *Idylls of the King* had appeared, and others were appearing. It was a red-letter evening indeed when the poet and new poem were ready for a reading, either in the little upstairs study, or in

the drawing-room, where dessert was always laid after dinner, and he sat at the head of the round table in a high carved chair . . .

They were magical evenings in which Tennyson cast over them his Arthurian spell, and they were bewitched by the sound of his 'God-gifted organ-voice', while through the drawing-room window they watched the light of the sunset suffusing the capes, sea and sky with pink and gold. And they could visualise Lyonnesse:

'A land of old upheaven from the abyss
By fire to sink into the abyss again;
Where fragments of forgotten people dwelt,
And the long mountains ended in a coast
Of ever-shifting sand, and far away
The phantom circle of a moaning sea'.

Thomas Carlyle found Emily to be a woman of great character, and in writing to his wife Jane, he commented: 'The first glance of her is the least favourable. A freckly round-faced woman, rather tallish and without shape, a slight lisp too . . . and unpromising at first glance; but she lights up bright glittering blue eyes when you speak to her; has wit, has sense, and were it not that she seems so very delicate in health, "sick without a disorder", I should augur well of Tennyson's adventure.' Marriage for Emily was equally as much an adventure as it was for Elizabeth Barrett Browning who had risen from a sick bed to marry the poet Robert Browning. Emily had suffered from back trouble all her life, and to have undertaken to marry Alfred at the age of thirty-seven required courage indeed, not only from the point of view of bearing children, but also in coping with the extremely active social life at Farringford. She was convinced she had married a great poet and was determined to record all his activities in a journal, so that her son, Hallam, when he came to write his *Memoir* of the poet, would have all the details at his finger-tips for future generations. She resolved to be another Dorothy Wordsworth who in her journal had immortalised her brother's activities in the Quantocks and the Lake District earlier that century.

The Farringford journal begins in October 1853, when together Emily and Alfred Tennyson travel down to the Isle of Wight to inspect the property they were to rent furnished for £2 weekly for three years before buying it in 1856:

Emily Tennyson's Farringford Journal Begins, 1853

October

Alfred [Tennyson] went to Bonchurch to his friends the James Whites, Edmund Peel & Feildens. From them he heard of Farringford as a place that might possibly do for us. He went and found it looking rather wretched with wet leaves trampled into the lawn. However we thought it worth while to go and look at it together. The railway did not go further than Brockenhurst then and the steamer, when there was one from Lymington, felt itself in no way bound to wait for the omnibus which brought as many of the passengers as it could from the train. We crossed in a rowing boat. It was a still November evening. One dark heron flew over the Solent backed by a daffodil sky.

We went to Lambert's, then Plumbley's Hotel . . . smaller than now. Next day we went to Farringford & looking from the drawing-room window thought 'I must have that view' and I said so to him when alone. So accordingly we agreed with Mr. Seymour to take the place furnished for a time on trial with the option of purchasing.

November

24th. We left Chapel House [Twickenham] to be occupied for the remainder of the lease by our Mother, and arrived at Lymington sleeping at the hotel as we feared to take our Hallam [born in 1852] over the Solent in a row-boat.

25th. A great day for us. We reached Farringford. It was a misty morning & two of the servants on seeing it burst into tears saying they could never live in such a lonely place. We amused ourselves during the autumn and winter by sweeping up leaves for exercise and by making a muddy path thro' the plantation into a Sandy one. We were delighted with the snowdrops & primroses in the plantation & by the cooing of the Stock-dove & the song of the Redwings.

1854

February

28th. He makes 'a bower of rushes' in the kitchen garden facing the down. Sitting there we heard the sound of the cannon practising for the Crimea. Their booming sounded somewhat knell-like. He found the little carriage in the village in which for so many years he drew me about when I could not walk – a constant source of pleasure to us.

March

16th. Our Lionel born. A. when he heard of it was watching in the little study under the bedroom and saw Mars in the Lion culminating. This afterwards determined us to give our baby the name of Lionel—a family name before proposed among others.

April

The little carriage was soon in requisition & I was taken by A. to see the 'wealth of Daffodils' in the wilderness and we admired the rose-coloured & green sheaths of the Lime leaves as they lay like flowers under the trees and a great many things besides. Edmund Lushington and Mr. Patmore had been staying with us about a week and they insisted on taking me up the down two days. The view delighted me and we were interested by a mirage which we saw on the top of the down as we ascended. There seemed a great river with black islands in it. All the air along the line of the down became visible in moving waves.

May

15th. The three gentlemen went up to London together.

23rd. A. returned.

25th. Mr. FitzGerald came & stayed about a fortnight. Delightfully amusing he was. He often went out with his sketch book and brought us home sketches and horn poppies and orchids and yellow Irises. In the evening he translated Persian odes for A. who had hurt his eye while I was shut up in my room by poring over a small printed

Persian Grammar which, with other Persian books whose type seemed to be trying, I confess to have hidden away. Some evenings Mr. FitzGerald played to us beautiful airs from Mozart, Handel, or some old English composer. His memory for music was wonderful.

June

3rd. Franklin Lushington came.

6th. Our Lionel was christened, he being one Godfather, Mr. FitzGerald standing proxy for Drummond Rawnsley & I for Emma Hamilton Russell who had been thrown out of a carriage & was confined to the sofa. On returning from Church we found Sir John Simeon. This was my first introduction to a friend who was to be so much to us both as long as he lived. A. had met him before.

Mr. Isaacson (the Rector), Mr. Bateman, Mr. Sheriff & a friend of his dined with us. Franklin Lushington made some sketches & left us on the 9th. He liked the place. When strong enough I helped A. to work in the garden. He took some very long walks in the great heat, to Bonchurch once and back, over the shingly shore, other walks almost as long to Newport & back & to Newtown. He knocked himself up but did not tell me.

July

25th. A letter from Edmund Lushington telling of his sister Louisa's death at Avignon on the 19th, a grievous loss. With the intellect of the family she had great sweetness and humility and was beloved by all.

The abundance of wild flowers was delightful to us. St. John's wort (a mystical plant as he called it), common centaury, common agrimony, the small campanula on the down, Law-wort, Flea-wort, & the lovely little Lady's tresses.

August

11th. We kept out little Hallam's birthday by taking him & our servants to Alum Bay. Hallam to his exceeding delight driving the donkey. Afterwards he was taken to Scratchell's Bay in a boat, A. & the servants with him. I had to go home with nurse & baby.

12th. I saw A. off on the Solent with Mr. Grant for Christchurch, Corfe Castle, Swanage. Near there they found an old Waterloo man who delighted them. They slept at Bournemouth one night, then Mr. Grant was obliged to return. A. went on to Glastonbury, Wells, Cheddar Cliffs, and came home on the 21st and was ill afterwards.

29th. Mr. Mundy came and we had a pleasant talk about Lincolnshire people. He left the next day.

September

1st. Sir John & Lady Simeon came to luncheon bringing his brother & sister, Baron de Schroeter, and Aubrey de Vere & all except Lady Simeon & myself went to Alum Bay & then in a boat to the Needles taking Hallam with them.

The Baron interested us greatly. His ardent love for souls being so rare.

6th. Aubrey de Vere comes to stay with us & Franklin Lushington, Edmund being also here.

We saw a great deal at this time of Baron de Schroeter, Aubrey de Vere, & the Simeons and had frequent and long conversations on Romanism. Our friends made a beautiful Temple of the Ugly Cavern full of half-hidden pits which Keenan's Catechism pictures to us. Still we remained true to our church. The Grants were also frequent and welcome guests. Mr. Palgrave also who made one of our pleasant circle at this time; he had brought Laurence's Portrait with him, now lent, afterwards given to me.

20th. The battle of Alma. A. read his 'Maud' to Sir John. The down was a constant source of enjoyment to all, including little Hallam & the Reef showed itself to greatest advantage.

October

10th. We read full particulars of the battle of Alma and touching letters from soldiers. Great disappointment darkened England on learning that the news that Sebastopol had fallen was false. Painful tidings of the Arctic Expedition.

13th. A moment of great excitement came when we saw flags flying and heard guns firing but it proved that the flags were only in honour of a Coast guard wedding. He read to Mr. de Vere & a party from

Swainston 'The Golden Year', 'Edwin Morris', Audley Court', & 'The Gardener's Daughter'. On the 31st Mr. de Vere leaves us. He had made the great change which had been discussed with so much interest in the little garden of Chapel House & seemed happy. Hallam shows an eager interest in the stars, insisting on being taken from window to window to look at them and doing his best to say 'twinkle, twinkle'.

He reads many of Campbell's poems, some of which he had read to me on the little yellow sofa near one of the drawing-room windows at Somersby & I said that if I lived to teach the boys, the patriotic songs should be among the first they should learn.

November

1st. Mr. Moxon comes and when told that friends wanted the Poems now nearly ready for publication to be published at once, he kindly urged that they should be regardless of trouble to himself. He left next day. Almost daily ascents of the Down helped by the Campstool, Mr. de Vere's gift to me.

8th. Looking from the Beacon and seeing the White Cliffs reflected in the beautifully clear sea, their violet gray shading looked to us tender & sad. Perhaps the landscape seemed so sad for the sorrowful news of the death in the trenches of the pious neighbour Colonel Hood.

14th. We read that touching account of the Scots Greys & Inniskillings how they [comported] themselves at Balaclava. The writer says that their 'ears are frenzied by the monotonous, incessant cannonade going on for days together'. Some Captain compares the appearance of the troops to the turning of a shoal of mackerel. We are almost afraid to open the newspapers now. Every day we go up the down or sweep up leaves & burn them. Sir John, Mr. Edmund Peel & Mr. & Mrs. Augustus Peel come. Mr. Millais comes on the 22nd and is beguiled into sweeping up leaves & burning them in the intervals of making sketches of Hallam & myself.

25th. He leaves. We have had talks as to the limits of realism in painting. A. hates overrealism . . .

[Gap in Journal]

December

2nd. A. writes 'The Charge of the Light Brigade' & sent it to *The Examiner*. We hear of the dreadful storm at Balaclava on November 14th & are shocked to know of the loss of the winter clothing of the troops in the *Prince* & of so many transports besides & alas also of so many lives.

Souvestre's account of the Bretons interests us very much. Their glory in the name of Christians, the fact that their most popular songs are religious, that when the cholera was among them they would not listen to the doctors until they put their advice in a song set to a National Air strikes us much.

He reads some of Dante's *Inferno* to me & then Virgil's Hades. The thought of Russia & of our soldiers is so absorbing that Hallam's games are of Russia or he falls down & says, 'this is the way the Russians fall when they are killed'. He loves to talk of the poor soldiers who have no butter & no toast. He sings 'Rule Britannia' with great ardour & is always asking for pictures of her. His love for her has almost superseded that of the stars tho' he does look at them still.

A. reads Homer's Hades to me. We read Ferrier's* *Institutes of Metaphysics.*

We keep Christmas by his blowing bubbles for the children who have pretty wreaths of laurel & holly on their heads. He is invited to meet his friends at the Grange but cannot go. Mr. Palgrave & his brother at the Hotel & often with us. Charles Weld also comes from Pondwell.

1855

January

10th. A. reads 'Maud'.

12th. Poems from Hazlitt's *Selection.* Mr. Tuckerman & his brother, pleasant Americans, bring a note of introduction from Mr. Robertson once a clergyman at Boxley. On coming up to the house they see a

*James Frederick Ferrier (1808-64), Professor of Civil History at Edinburgh, and later of moral philosophy and political economy at St. Andrews.

yellow light strong enough to cast their shadows & those of the trees. No Aurora & no meteor visible but the clouds slightly luminous, the night otherwise pitchy dark. The Tuckermans dine two or three days & walk & talk. It's interesting to see how they cling to the thought of the old English home . . .

Day by day we are saddened by the seemingly hopeless news from the Crimea. Such terrible incapacity & neglect judging from the *Times* & also partly from private accounts.

A robin in the house so tame that it let me take it in my hand & when A. was reading to me it sat near us by the fire.

February

1st. Very cold, the snow folding in & out of the hedge like drapery. A. reads some of the *Idylls* of Theocritus to me. 'Hylas', 'The Ile of Cos', & 'The Syracusan Women', also the first poem of 'Maud' in the rough.

Whirling snow in the driving east wind. One of the finest American Pines half blown down. He read some of Edgar Poe's Poems to me two or three evenings, then the beginning of 'Maud' & the Mad Song and one night all 'Maud'.

Our poor little Lionel has been suffering from Eczema after vaccination. The golden mist of Hallam's hair and 'ruby-budded limes' [from *Maud* part IV, i;] and notice of six volumes of *Punch* bound, the gift of Messrs. Bradbury & Evans [publishers], cheer the wintry weather.

A. reads *Othello* to me in three nights, then two Acts of *Macbeth,* then finished *Macbeth* & read *Richard III* in three evenings. Afterwards *Henry IV* . . . We liked to hear the Shrove Tuesday ditty of the Village children about white bread, fat bacon, apple pie, Mother's Day & other things that could not be made out by us. Lionel delights in warlike songs. In one of our rash walks up the down A. got a chill & was very unwell . . .

Mr. Woolner came & on the 5th began A.'s Medallion.

16th. The Crocus wreath began to burn.

19th. Mr. Woolner left. I thought the medallion very beautiful, very fine & shiny, the best likeness that has been made.

Mr. Woolner leaves on the 19th. He gives Hallam a bit of Virgin gold from Australia. 'Loola' was very kind to him & was a great darling with him.

21st. Fast day, so stormy we could not go to church nor get out at all except that A. breathed the air for a few minutes.

March

Spring Birds & flowers duly chronicled, each one hailed with gladness. Each varied aspect of Down & sea giving fresh delight. A letter from Mr. Ruskin kindly asking A. to see his Turners, Mr. Woolner having spoken of his desire to see them. A. says to her 'cold and clear cut face' [from *Maud,* part III] and she had said 'Crown Imperial full of tears'.* View exquisitely beautiful. Snow sparkling in Blackgang.

30th. Heard the first Stock-Dove.

31st. He read a good deal of 'Maud' again.

April

2nd. A. finished Goethe's 'Helena' to me. We only admired the classical part & the lines, 'Dort hinten still im Gebirgtal hat' and 'Nicht nur Verdienst, auch Treue' and a little also the Vine chorus & Rock chorus.

3rd. Were to have gone to see the Baltic Fleet off but the storm of wind & rain prevented us. A letter comes from Mr. Tom Taylor announcing his intended marriage.

5th. We drive to Newport, he on his way to Bonchurch whence he returns on the 9th and tells me wonderful scientific facts of which he has heard from Dr. Mann. The one cowslip spared in the Park had been spared for his return.

Shakespeare several evenings. Anne Weld & Agnes stay a few days having come over from Pondwell with Mrs. Leacock & Mrs. Cuthbert, her sister-in-law, who returned the same day.

We accompany the Welds to Newport & go to Swainston. All there very kind & pleasant but we are bad guests for however gladly

---

*'Crown Imperial full of tears' refers to the species of flower called *Fritillaria imperialis,* which is red. Concealed in its head are black and white spots resembling tears. According to legend, when Jesus Christ was led away from the Garden of Gethsemane all the plants bowed their heads save this one, which, when it learned later of His crucifixion, wept bitterly, thereafter bearing the mark of those tears for evermore.

we welcomed our friends at home, they felt that our work and therefore our chief pleasure was there & that there we must for the part be. At Swainston they met Mr. Silvera, priest who interested them, & they were taken to see Sir Henry & Lady Mary Gordon [of Northcourt, Shorwell] who were not at home but the Housekeeper who had been Miss Gordon's nurse took them over the chief rooms and about the grounds pointing out the oaks her young lady had planted & taking all the hearty delight in everything belonging to the family so seldom found now. They were charmed with the old rooms & the oriel windows looking out on the grassy terrace with the pretty village church whose tower & spire were seen from among the fir trees or in the near sloping park or the more distant down. Mr. Godley dined with us at Swainston. Hallam & Johnnie wild with delight, Hallam much the wildest. Lady Simeon ill in bed but Sir John kindly insisted on taking us to see Mr. Nun's beautiful flowers.

25th. A. read 'Maud' in the morning & we go home afterwards. He reads to me some of Wiseman next evening, some of 'The Lady of the Lake', Primrose, rose-coloured sheath of the Sycamore leaves, Cuckoos, Nightingales, all sights and sounds of April delighted us. I write out 'Maud'.

May

1st. We hear of Franklin Lushington's appointment to a judgeship in Corfu. We admire the deep-red catkins hanging from the topmost branches of the Black Poplar against the blue sky. Also the white glistening buds of the Elms.

The end of the Chapel House lease had come & we put away books & papers & go to Twickenham, parting[?] to Cowes. We call on old friends there . . .

[The Tennysons leave for London, to view the Great Exhibition at the Crystal Palace. They travel on to Oxford, where Alfred is to receive his doctorate of letters. They walk in Christ Church meadows, and inspect the stars through the powerful telescope at the Radcliffe observatory. 'I had first seen Oxford when six years old . . . when a summer's sunset gilded the domes & churches. Then it seemed a fairy city to me and now it looked like a dream of the Middle Ages'. They returned to the Island via London.]

July

7th. We reach home again. 'Maud' was finished which added to the delight of returning.

8th. A. reads [me] one of Jowett's Essays, a gift which we found on our return. We had brought Stanley's gift with us too that pleased us much. We went to Swainston & found the Goldschmidts on the road coming to us.

Mr. Lear and Mr. Peel came to us & Mr. Bradley called, the beginning of our acquaintance with this good and able and affectionate friend.

The wealth of wild flowers is a continual source of delight to us. We filled a bowl with orchis—like sunrise, as he said, and with campanula & other wonderful flowers which could rival any bowl filled from a greenhouse as we thought. We saw a green thing like a grasshopper, 2½ inches long. It had bright green wings.

My Father came & next day, August 6th, we take the children to the Warren to call on the Bradleys, & see Mrs. Bradley for the first time. She was preparing tea among the furze bushes to celebrate her little girl Edith's birthday.

August

6th. He sends the 'Balaclava Charge' to be printed for the soldiers as they want it & the Chaplain of the S.P.G. tells that we could not do a greater service than to send them copies on slips. We sent 2,000 slips, I think, & they are to have another 1,000 if wanted.

A. reads Margaret Fuller to me. We keep Hallam's birthday by an expedition to Brook ourselves & our servants. A beautiful day. Stock-doves cooing continually in the morning. A letter from Mr. Lear giving little hope of Henry Lushington's life.

13th. My Father left us & we went on the down, saw more butterflies I thought than I had seen in my whole life together before. The Mundys who were still at the hotel had seen a great many just before, dead, and [several] large brown ones abounded in the lower lanes. We began *Margherita Pustula.* On the 14th we heard from Edmund Lushington of his brother Henry's death at Paris. A great loss to all. His brother Franklin had arrived too late to see him alive. A. reads 'Ecclesiastes' to me which he had once read to Henry Lushington, also 'Solomon's Song'.

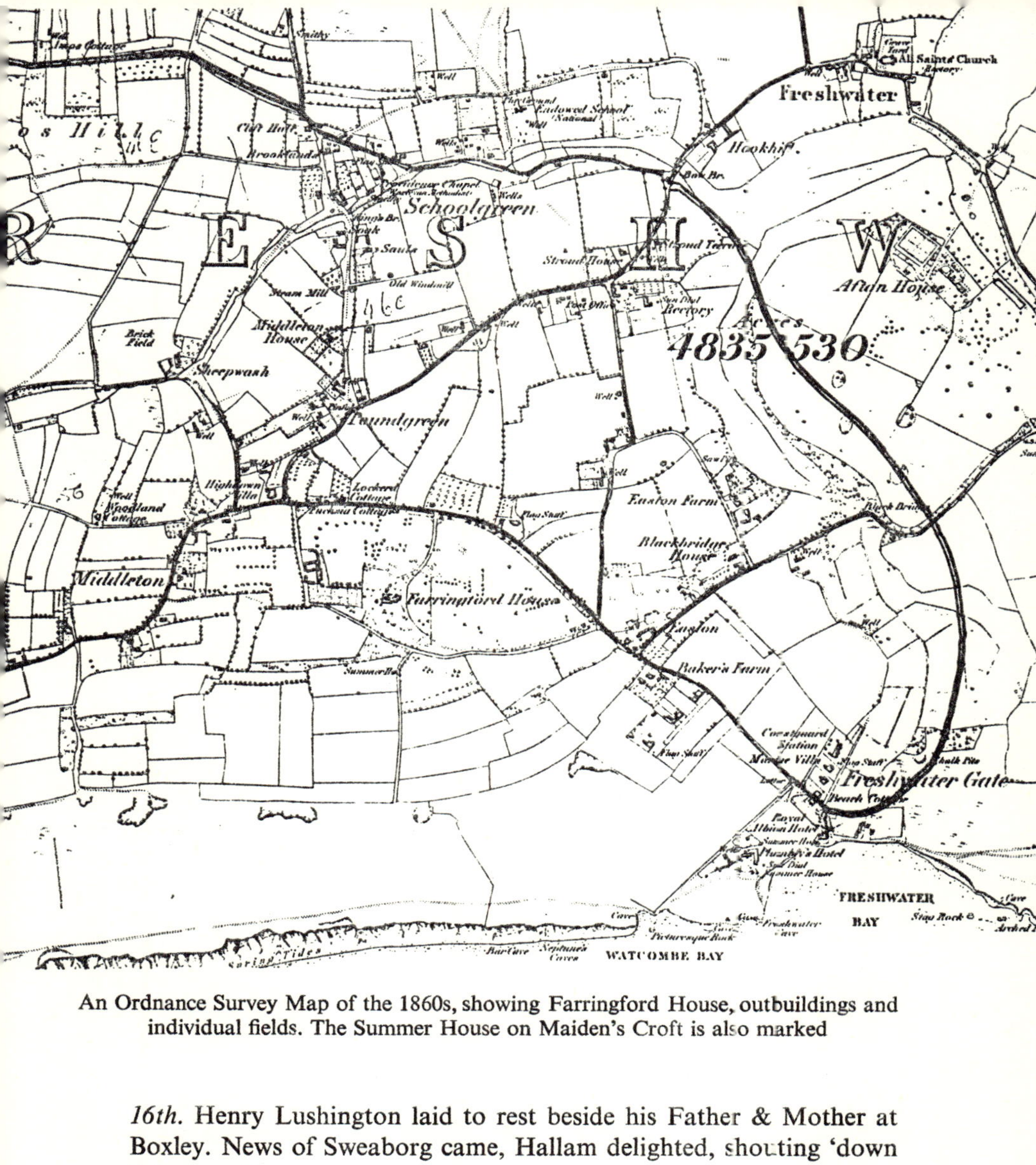

An Ordnance Survey Map of the 1860s, showing Farringford House, outbuildings and individual fields. The Summer House on Maiden's Croft is also marked

16th. Henry Lushington laid to rest beside his Father & Mother at Boxley. News of Sweaborg came, Hallam delighted, shouting 'down Sebastapol'.

18th. News of the French & Sardinian Victory on the Tchernaya. I at last enjoyed a scramble over the rocks from Colwell Bay to Totland with the Mundys who were staying with us now. At their request A. reads 'The Charge of the Light Brigade' to them & afterwards the 'Ode to the Duke of Wellington' & some of Campbell's Songs.

19th. A. reads the last hours of Oliver Cromwell to them. Next day the Mundys leave. We examine a quicksilver fly thro' the microscope, also a cocoon which looks like a honeycomb of burnished silver, the eggs like the crumbs of Whiters bread.

A great thunderstorm, Blackgang Chine ghostly white in the moonlight, a grand black thunderous cloud between the moon & the glorious paths of moonlight. On the sea lightening round the horizon and then in many coloured fire all over the heavens. There was a hollow voice in the thunder & the storm lasted many hours.

Next night the moon came up over the down & he said it was like Michael Angelo's sunrise in the Medici Chapel at Florence. The head over the giant shoulder.

29th. A. left for the Peak & I taught Hallam for the first time to say his prayers.

September

3rd. A. returned in an open boat, the bow slapping the wave each time it falls, the sea being very rough.

We went to meet him but he had not arrived by the steamer, the hour of which had been changed, but, tho' I asked both postman & Captain, neither told me this but left me sick at heart not finding him. After his long ramble in the Forest & his rough passage he had to walk home for there was no Fly. However he arrived at last. He had not been to the Peak but had enjoyed his week at Salisbury . . . & in the New Forest. This last most of all. His descriptions of the fire of the sun in the Fern, a background to the boles of the great Beeches; of the purple glow of the heath & of the delicious heath air all of which I love so dearly revived my old wish to see the Forest. In a clear & rather rapid stream he had seen a cow standing with cataracts of light from the four legs. In one old part of the New Forest he had found the ground under the trees quite covered with leaves of wood sorrel. In other parts the ground was bare, in others covered with beautiful grass.

4th. I was walking in the garden with Hallam after A. had gone in when Mr. & Mrs. Frederick Pollock drove up & introduced themselves to me. They had dined & so went to Alum Bay while we dined and came to us in the evening & got him to read some of 'Maud'. Having unpacked their things at the Hotel they slept there and came next morning after breakfast. We sat in our reed hut in the kitchen garden and after a time he finished 'Maud'. The Pollocks dined with us at luncheon & they returned to their children.

Next day the Grants came to High Down Villa, a red house built during our absence from home, a most unwelcome sight opposite our Farm Gate. However the Grants were welcome inhabitants. So able & cultivated & friendly a man as Mr. Grant could not be otherwise than a delightful neighbour.

Mr. Palgrave, also ever a welcome guest, arrives next day & we walked with him & the Grants, one or more, dined with us from time to time. We had interesting conversation. We superintended trimming a thorn to open a view of Brook point and took Hallam up to the down & built chalk towers & demolished them, 'the smoke' giving exceeding delight to the little boy.

On the 9th with joy & thankfulness checked in part by past false reports, we heard of the fall of Sebastapol. This time the report was official. After dinner at which Mr., Mrs., & Miss Grant and also Mr. Stokes & Miss Cotton, as well of course as our guest Mr. Palgrave, were present, he read 'The Tapestried Chamber' & being in high spirits he made every one very merry with his talk.

17th. Mr. Palgrave went & A. read 'Maud' in walks on the down, the sound of the stock-doves' wings among the trees in the Park as he lay on the seat under the Cedar, a beautiful sound. A. read some of the *Symposium* to me in the evening. A very happy evening. Next day after a glorious walk on the down he read the new poem in 'Maud'.

The day after Mr. Grant & his friend Mr. Porte called & asked us all to go out with them in a boat. We all went & found the sea so very rough as we neared the point that we did not round it but hoisted sail & returned. The sky was bright & the waves fine & the old sailor's humorous remarks amused us.

Pleasant walks & pleasant evenings with Mr. Grant & Mr. Porte.

24th. Miss Grant takes leave.

25th. A. went to the dentist in London, Mr. Grant & Mr. Porte with him as far as Basingstoke. Lady Grant tells me that she has planted a bit of myrtle which A. gave her meeting her in the hall one day when she dined here & that she had given a bit to Miss Grant & also to a Shropshire lady. He will be quite ashamed of having so much made of his little bit of myrtle. In obedience to his wish that I should not miss my daily walk I go up the down day by day & I am very sorry that he should not see the splendid harvest moon.

27th. He dined at the Brownings & had a very pleasant time. Read 'Maud'. The two Rossettis came in the evening.

Lady Grant tells me that Sir Graham Hamond had charmed his eighteen guests into sitting intent while he read them 'The Charge of the Six Hundred' which she had taken him & had not seen before. Also she told how one cold winter's morning Sir John Simeon had repeated it to the Hunters waiting on some hill for the scent or something else, & how they all listened & seemed to forget what they had come there [for].

30th. Thanksgiving Day. So rainy no one could go to church so I read the Prayer appointed for the day at evening prayers at home. He dined with the Camerons & met Mr. Brookfield, Mr. Spedding, Mrs. Bayley & Miss Crawford and read 'Maud'.

October

1st. He dined at the Welds and enjoyed looking at his sketches in Brittany. Mr. Spedding & Frederic were also there.

2nd. He arrived about half nine from Cowes, our usual route in those days. A Mr.—comes from Nottingham to see him, an Artisan. We ask him to dinner. He wants to hear some of 'Maud'. A. reads all. We fear that the poor man must have been hurt that we knew nothing of his poems which he had sent. They had been acknowledged and one reads something of every book to see if it ought to be read & then if it seems that it ought not, one throws it aside & it is forgotten but not without a pang thinking how much it has cost the writer and what high hopes have perhaps been built upon it. One really could do nothing else but read small books of poems & pass judgment on them if one read all sent. The very letter writing takes not unfrequently till 2 or 3 or even four o'clock in the day and all to no purpose save that of courtesy as far as the stranger part goes. But we were sorry for this pilgrim from a distant county. He was very good about the matter.

The saddest incident (rather most tragic) of this kind was one at Chapel House [Twickenham] when an old Waterloo Soldier brought his twelve books on the battle of Waterloo. He had taught himself to read & write (I believe that he might write these). He wanted to know if they should be published. 'Great images loomed' sometimes thro' words of the old man's creation but A. was obliged to say that 'they could not be published as a whole' but that Publishers might accept parts for magazines. The dear old soldier came & carried away his twelve books in their oak case (I think it was). We asked him to come & see us but he never came again.

At this time we have the pleasure of seeing again a good deal of the Swainston party. One day we had an exciting slide down to Alum Bay, the clay path wet from recent storms. We came up with our feet in eel baskets. The Kents are with the Simeons. Milton, part of Hallam, Carlyle's *Cromwell,* our evening readings now.

14th. A letter from the Senior Chaplain (Crimea) asking for a thousand more copies of 'The Charge'. A. reads part of *King John* to me.

17th. Franklin Lushington & Mr. Lear come. A long talk with F.L. in the morning then he walked with A. nearly all over the farm. Sir John Simeon comes with Mr. Deane. I forget Friday & fish which spoils my dinner, theirs being spoilt. However Mr. Lear's singing made us forget this whatever else it brought to mind. He sang for two or three hours. The whole of 'Mariana', the whole of 'The Lotos Eaters', 'Ellen Adair', 'Tears idle tears', 'Let the solid ground'. Then go by 'Oh that 'twere possible'. All his own settings. Next morning we breakfasted at half past six to see him & F.L. off. When they were gone we counted seven capes all glorious in the golden morning mist. Then we went up to the Attic & looked through the telescope to try & watch their boat & we thought we saw a boat & Mr. Lear said it must have been theirs for no other boat was crossing. I put F.L.'s 'Points of War' & his brother Henry's two poems to music. When we have given [up] Mrs. Cameron & Julia both, they arrive with their little German maid Katchen, all thro' the storm & the rain. A. reads to us some Milton. He is most good in reading to me in the evenings.

Next day while they had walked to the Light House, Sir John Simeon & Sir George Baker came. Sir John charmed with Mayall's photograph of A. which Mrs. Cameron had had framed & brought down, also Raphael's Maria which she had put into a starry frame. We talked all the evening speculative talk dear to A. & to me.

Next evening he reads some of Shakespeare's sonnets, two of Milton's, & others to us and next day after church part of *Samson Agonistes.* We go in the afternoon to church whenever able, the morning service being too long for my strength except on Communion Sundays when I go for that service only.

Visits to Afton & Norton made in a not very luxurious Donkey chaise. On one occasion Julia's foot having gone thro' the moment she stept into it. However we went merrily on.

Sir John & Lady Simeon & Sir George Baker came to dinner. The children were made to walk over the table, nothing loath. All very merry. Mrs. Cameron played on the piano & Julia sang & Sir John & A. made high shouldered ghosts. We wished for Aubrey de Vere. Strange to say a letter came from him next day. We were not frequent correspondents. Mrs. Cameron summoned hastily home by her little Charlie's illness.

One day we go up the down and are charmed by magical effects of cloud. Other days we sweep up leaves. He reads two or three of Edgar Poe's poems to me one evening, another an Essay in *The Westminster Review* on Intuitive Proof of God from design. The wild flight of birds delightful, walks up the down, sweeping leaves, evening reading, one night an interesting letter in *The Times,* another part of *The London Review* on 'Maud'.

Kind letters from Mr. Ruskin & Mr. Tuckerman.

A. reads me some of Thackeray's *Humourists of England.* By A.'s desire I read *The Newcomes.* Some parts I grant tender & beautiful but others seemed to me heart-withering & I do not wonder that there is no youth among the young now if this is the food on which they feed.

After sweeping of leaves & burning them in which Hallam, happy boy, joins, we play at Backgammon . . . to spare his eyes from reading, but he generally reads to me a little first. Another kind letter from Mr. Ruskin, but he does not accept A.'s invitation to visit us, only says he should like it.

December

8th. Very cold but we go to church notwithstanding. He reads some of St. John & Jowett's Essay on the Atonement.

Burn leaves & dig & put sand & ashes in the shrubbery.

12th. We make a bonfire of leaves & burn the box with all the pipes in it, he having first put the last bit of tobacco into his study fire-thinking that he would give up smoking.

An Italian comes with his Hurdy-gurdy & when we had given him some money, he asked if he might come & warm himself by the fire. We talked a little in Italian to him & he told us he came from Genoa. A letter from Mr. Brimley. An interesting one from Mr. W[oolner] telling of a relation who had been roused from a state of despondency by 'The Two Voices'. He came to Ryde for change and on the evening of his arrival saw for the first time A.'s poems. He read 'The Two Voices', burst into tears & soon returned quite restored to his family.

I read some of Plutarch's 'Theseus' to A. in Langhorne's *Lives* for we said we must read these Lives.

Mr. Brodie comes by Mr. Monteith's desire to make a bust of A. Very cold weather.

15th. A. goes to Newport to consult Sir John Simeon about our own affairs. He as ever most kind.

19th. Mr. Grant & Mr. Jowett come. Still very cold.

20th. Too cold for me to join their walk.

21st. Mr. Brodie goes. A. reads 'Maud'.

23rd. Mr. Palgrave arrives. A., Mr. Jowett, & Mr. Grant go to church. A. reads some Milton.

24th. We put up Holly & evergreens in the rooms. Mr. Stokes dines with us; Mr. Grant's cousins, the two Miss Cottons & their brothers, & Miss Way, their cousin, come in the evening. The circle becomes formal & A. insists on a game of Blindman's buff so we had a good child's game of English Blindman's buff which I for my part enjoyed. A great thunderstorm to-day & there had been one before in the night.

27th. Mr. Jowett & Mr. Grant & Mr. Palgrave leave us. A very pleasant time we have had with them. Many interesting talks. Mr. Palgrave lent us Macaulay to read & *Esmond* & Mr. Grant gave A. Lewes's *Goethe*,[1] and Keightley's *Milton* & *Hiawatha*.[2] They were also most kind in bringing the children books & toys & in playing at ball with both & in having all manner of gambols with Hallam in which baby was too young to join.

28th. Charles Weld came to us while we were in the plantation having walked from Newport. He read us 'A Pardon' from his tour in Brittany which interested us.

29th. He read 'Carnac'[3], also interesting.

30th. A. & I went to church.

31st. To-day he had to go [to] the Grange.

---

1. George Henry Lewes, *The Life and Works of Goethe*, 1855.

2. Thomas Keighley, *The Fairy Mythology*, 1850.

3. Carnac, on the coast of Brittany, by the Bay of Quiberon; famous for its numerous prehistoric stone monuments and remains of early settlement.

1856

January

1st. A letter from him written at Southampton & enclosing Mr. Jowett's kind letter received just as he was starting. This makes my New Year's day happy just as I had been saying to myself 'It is dreary without him'. Charles makes a kite for the children to their exceeding delight. Lionel asks if Hallam will go to the sky with a string. I try in vain to secure some pleasant companion for Charles. He leaves me on the 2nd & I am very sorry that he should have had so dull a visit.

My daily letter from A., even on the 8th when he returns.

4th. A very kind letter also from Mr. Brookfield telling about him. During his absence there was a wonderful meteor over the Solent, but I did not see it.

9th. He read me some of Eckermann's conversations with Goethe. We are very cozy in the Study with the large screen across the window. We are still brave enough to go up the down sometimes.

15th-17th. Mr. Estcourt comes to look over the place for us with a view of our purchasing. Merwood walks with us. A beautiful bright day. Molière these evenings and a little Eckermann. A. goes out at night.

18th. We learn that Russia has accepted the proposals of peace. The Sardinian comes again. In the evening [read some of] De Quincey about the death of his sister. The children much excited by the stranding of a ship near Brook. A. carves some ivy leaves from nature in Apple-tree wood. In spite of its hardness they are very well carved. They are now moulded in pottery at Middleton Farm doorways.

20th. After church in the afternoon he reads to me about the London Poor.

22nd. Sir John Simeon fetches A. to Swainston.

24th. He looks in at the Drawing-room window having returned to me while Sir John is at Ryde. He tells me of the Saxon king found in his tunic, a net work of gold & of Romans & Saxons lying side by side in the same tombs of the last Roman barrow made on the downs, a barrow still tho' clothed with grass; of the last fires in the British hearth seen when the soil is turned up a little.

Hallam very pleased to see Papa. The two children sat beside as we dined.

25th. I walk with him on his way to Swainston. As it is the first time I have appeared on the road my appearance causes some excitement.

Walked in the fields & met Merwood who asked me about plowing the orchard. I say that I will write to A. Merwood is an idyllic sort of man, he can neither read nor write. He is very shrewd. I talk to him sometimes about farming matters. A peace comes to one from the quiet here and one feels it good to have one's home & I hope feels thankful for the beautiful home tho' I for my part should prefer one on some heathy hill on the mainland when I think of the difficulty of getting to my Father if he were ill.

Finished Macaulay & read some of Eckermann. Letters from A. who is now at Ventnor with the Manns. He has seen Saturn pretty

Ruins of Tennyson's Summer House, looking towards Freshwater Bay

well. All the rings seemed to him one except the dark ring where it crossed the bright.

February

1st. He tells me of the beautiful octuple system in Orion which to the naked eye looks like rather a faint star under the lower star in Orion's belt.

4th. He comes home while I am on the Down. We read part of *The Misanthrope* together. A. had been going to copy [Simeon's] lovely passage on young children but Sir John lends him the book for me. A. reads me the picture of Nimuë (Vivien) & Merlin.*

5th. Up the down. He reads me that book of *The Odyssey* about the dead.

6th. We dig or rather hoe in the garden. He begins *The Odyssey* to me. I feel that in his beautiful *viva voce* translations, quite literal, I get as much as it is possible to have of the true spirit of the original.

7th. Rainy & stormy, we do not get out. While we are playing with the children in the drawing room, Mr. Woolner arrives about the second book of *The Odyssey* in the evening. We have in these days two or three pleasant walks & every evening *The Odyssey.* Lady Simeon & Miss Simeon call.

16th. A. & Mr. Woolner dine at Swainston.

19th. Sir John returns with them to dinner & likes Mr. Woolner's medallion of me.

22nd. We send a servant to Chapel House to look to the packing of our furniture.

24th. A. reads Lowth's Isaiah.

A. takes me out when the days are sunny & I sit in the arbor.

Mr. Woolner most kind to the children.

28th. The bust looks nearly finished. Difficult work for Mr. Woolner as A. is not at all fond of having his face copied & will only spare a little while at night when Mr. Woolner has to take a candle in one hand & model as he can.

The snow-drops are beautiful & the Russian violets which A. brought from Steephill castle thriving & deliciously sweet.

---

*'Enid and Nimuë: or the True and the False', which was printed in 1857 but never published as such.

29th. We have been waiting more than six weeks for a decisive answer about the price of this place. We long for a settled home & in spite of the difficulty of getting to & from this, we like it too well to wish to leave it . . .

March

1st. A. finishes *The Odyssey.* I very sorry it is done.

2nd. He reads the book of Esther and a good deal more from the Bible.

4th. He began *Hamlet.* He digs in the garden every day.

5th & 6th. Hamlet.

7th & 8th. As you Like It.

9th. He reads 'The Sermon on the Mount' and a good deal besides in the Bible.

10th. Mr. Butler calls. We ask him to dinner & he comes. He admires the bust which is finished.

11th, 12th, 13th. Twelfth Night.

13th. Much Ado About Nothing.

14th. Mr. Butler dines & A. reads 'Maud'.* A. digs almost every day & sometimes walks with Mr. Woolner. I not well enough.

15th. Mr. Woolner leaves us. A. finishes *Much Ado.*

16th. Our Lionel's birthday. Mrs. Cameron sends, 'The Poems in Memoriam & Maud' beautifully bound to Hallam thinking it his. Poor little Lionel had only our small gifts, and for sport bubbles blown which pleased both children much. Hallam ran after 'the beautiful birds' with great glee and opal worlds which burst leaving nothing but smoke behind half awed them both.

---

*It may be of interest to note the receipts from Mr. Moxon, Tennyson's publishers, between 1850 and 1860; as taken from *Materials for a Life of A.T.* by Hallam Tennyson:

1851 – £747
1852 – £757
1853 – £1658
1855 – £445 (the Crimea War sent down the value of the book)
1856 – £2058 (after publication of *Maud*)
1858 – £1299
1859 – £928
1860 – £4542 (after publication of *Idylls of the King*)

(10,000 copies of these *Idylls of the King* were sold in the first week of publication).

17th. A. began *Measure for Measure* in the evening. He walked alone on the down the harshest wind being too much for me.

The 18th brought a petition for a National Song for Wales. I obliged to order our furniture to be warehoused because we cannot get an answer about this place.

19th. Heard the Stock dove for the first time this year. A. said the exquisite song to me from 'Merlin' (Vivien). He has set to work in earnest on the poem now. Wind changed to N.W. after having been so long in the East. *Measure for Measure* this evening.

20th & 21st. 'Merlin'.

24th. Mr. Venables, Mr. & Mrs. Tom Taylor arrive. Delightful Beethoven from her & some settings of A.'s songs.

25th. Mr. Richard Doyle arrives & Sir John Simeon dines with us. Mr. Doyle had a stormy passage in an open boat & lost his hat. He wrapt himself in his plaid & the woman screams at the gray ghost when he goes to buy a hat. The steamer had gone to look at the gun boats. A. & the Taylors see them first near the Needles like wild fowl on the water. Mr. Venables took cold yesterday & did not join in the walk but stayed with me & we talked for hours. A delightful companion he is. Mrs. Taylor sings her own settings of some of A's poems. 'The Sisters', 'The Miller's Daughter', 'The Brook' are what we like best. A great gift for music she has.

26th. The Taylors and Mr. Doyle go to see the hounds throw off at Swainston. A. & Mr. Venables walk over later. All return in the evening.

27th. A. got cold yesterday & so does not join in the walk to Brook, has a warm bath instead. Miss Cottons & Miss Way in the evening. Music again.

28th. Sir John Simeon & Mr. Pollen dine with us & Dr. & Mrs. Mann come in the evening. Our guests walked to Alum Bay & home by Totland Bay before dinner.

30th. A. reads 'Merlin' ('Vivien') to Mr. Venables & me in the Study. I am glad that he agrees with me in thinking it so grand.

31st. Sir John Simeon & Mr. Pollen come with Mr. Estcourt. Mr. Pollen & Dr. Mann walk to the Needles & delight to watch the sea birds. Meanwhile we have a grand consultation with Mr. Venables & Sir John about Farringford. They had kindly given up the Hunt to help. Most kind both of them. Both wish us to buy it. Mr. & Mrs.

Taylor leave us. Sir John takes the rest of the party to Swainston except Dr. & Mrs. Mann who come to stay with us. We are sorry to lose our pleasant guests.

April

1st. Dr. & Mrs. Mann work in their own room. I too tired to do anything. We have some of the Essay in the evening.

3rd. They go. We dine early with them & talk in the evening.

4th. He takes me out in the garden a little & reads 'Merlin'. I read 'Enid & Geraint' to myself before. We hear the Stock Dove in the Elm . . .

9th. A. brings me white violets & primroses. Mr. Grant comes unexpectedly. Comes again in the evening & hears 'Merlin' after I have gone to bed. He gives me Robertson's 'Sermons' & brings Blake's 'Job', a gift to A. from Mr. Jowett.

10th. A. finishes writing out 'Merlin' and gives it to me to read. I read one of Robertson's sermons and like it much. Mr. Grant comes while we are in the garden and wheels ashes in the wheelbarrow for A. A. & I talk in the evening.

11th. He reads me the beginning of the first book of King Arthur. Three days following I have read 'Merlin' to myself, also some of Matthew Arnold's poems and Browning's.

12th. He reads some of the *Purgatorio.* A. plants potatoes. I watch. Mr. Sheriff calls to take leave. We read Robertson's sermons and like them very much. Mr. Grant dines with us & walks with A. at night.

14th. A letter from Mr. Estcourt saying that Mr. Seymour accepts our terms.

16th. A. brings me a little bit of the first of the *Idylls of the King* (*Geraint and Enid*) I walked in the garden while he was planting Potatoes. In the evening he reads me some of *La Mare au Diable.* A most kind invitation to Coniston from the Marshalls.

17th. Read Robertson's *Sermons* & Johnson's *Chemistry of Common Life,* write letters as usual, & between while I make manuscript books for him. I walk in the garden while he digs. Read some of *Hiawatha.* We send for Merwood to know the rent of the orchard & beg him not to let doves & other birds be shot. He told me that I had my wish of Rooks building in the trees for some had built there. He reads some *La Mare au Diable*. Mr. Grant comes about seven & tells us that he has to go next week about the Chair of Moral Philosophy. The Plum tree which fell in the winter, tho' only attached by a little bit of bark to the soil, is blossoming as if it were in the ground. A. & I planted the Barberry which we had brought with us.

19th. We re-potted the oleanders & planted the large Alexandrian laurel, which had years ago been given me from Wrangle, near our bower.

21st. Aunt Franklin & Sophy Cracroft drive over from Cowes & return after dinner. Sir John & Lady Simeon hail us in the down lane but cannot stay because they brought Johnnie & baby. Mr. Grant stayed to dinner. Drummond Rawnsley arrives.

22nd. Our servants went thro' the Fleet arrayed for the Review to-morrow & were charmed with the day.

23rd. We set off about half past seven with Drummond & Mr. Grant for Yarmouth with a wretched white pony and we feared we should be too late but in reaching the Toll bar we saw other carriages & the little *Solent* just coming out of the Lymington river. The Simeons with Mr. Godley and Mr. Wynn and Sir James Carmichael, the Croziers, Hamonds, A. Court Holmes, Captain were also on board. All very kind. The sea was calm & the passage to Yarmouth seemed short. We steamed past the stately ships & the gun boats & the block ships & the floating batteries all dressed with their wreath of flags. The yellow sands swarmed with people clustering like bees. Here & there red coats enlivened the mass. The *Victory* stood up proudly in the midst of the harbour. We heard a salute, then the *Victory* manned arms and soon the Royal Yacht with its three tall masts each bearing a flag came out of harbour. Every ship saluted. The smoke curled along the whole line six miles long, I was told, & then cleared partly away & we saw the ships & the distant hills beginning to appear. A beautiful sight. Soon the Queen's Yacht passed us & the ships manned arms & we heard the cheer of the *British Tar* and the *Solent* cheered too. It was pleasant to hear A.'s voice cheering. I waved my handkerchief. As we passed at the head of the lines I thought of the avenue of Sphinxes, the great ships stood so still and grand. But at times one could not help wishing for the old sails. We steamed along behind the Queen's Yacht. The two hours of the royal luncheon seemed long but then came a magnificent sight. The whole fleet passed the Queen, wheeled round the Pivot Ship & returned. The Pivot ships looked grand with their yards manned. All through the Review we caught now & then distant sounds of 'God Save the Queen'. As we returned the gun boats were attacking Southsea Castle. A cloud of smoke with occasional flashes. The sound was to our ears surprisingly little both of this and of the salutes but in reality so great that it shook the windows at Farringford. Now came the parting salute to the Queen & then we steamed back to Yarmouth & arrived about nine at home & found a pretty tea set out on the round table in the drawing room with hot meats on a side table. Sir John with his friends, Mr. Wynn, Mr. Godley & Sir James Carmichael, in addition to our own party. I am glad we have seen this great sight, glad too that it was on St. George's Day & Shakespeare's birthday. It was pleasant to watch the enjoyment of the little Simeons & A. Court Holmes. I see Louisa & Mary Simeon to-day for the first time (Two dear friends to be). I longed for my Father who was himself to have been a sailor. How he would have delighted in the day.

24th. Drummond walks on Afton down with A. & hears a few lines of King Arthur & is shown the new poem in 'Maud'. We dined early with him & he walks afterwards to the Ferry. Mr. Grant in the evening.

25th. A hue & cry after his new great coat. I fear it was lost in the boat. He has to go to Oxford without it. We hope soon to see him again. A. read me the Peleus of Catullus all except the Fates. Merwood came to tell us of white sand which he thought would do for glass-making. Afterwards he brought some lime & told us of building stone and the best chalk pit of the place all on our land. I went in to attend to A.'s warm bath & afterwards Mr. Watson arrived with his two daughters bringing a letter from Norton Lodge. They asked to look over the place where they had spent a happy year. I showed the girls all the rooms.

We have heard the Chiff Chaffs two or three days.

29th. A. reads me some of *Troilus & Cressida* and makes letters with bricks for our Hallam.

30th. This morning a letter comes from Mr. Venables saying that Mr. Chapman pronounces the title of Farringford good. We have agreed to buy, so I suppose it is ours. Went to our withy bed, such beautiful blue hyacinths, orchises, marsh marigolds and cowslips.

Wild cherry trees too with single white blossom. The park has for many days been rich with cowslips and furze in flower. The elms are a golden wreath at the foot of the down, we admired the mespilus in flower and the apple trees with their rosy buds. He dug the bed ready for the rhododendrons. A thrush was singing among the other birds, as he said 'mad with joy'. At sunset the burning splendour of Blackgang Chine, and St. Catherine's, and the red bank of the primeval river contrasted with the turquoise blue of the sea (that is our view from the drawing-room) make altogether, a miracle of beauty. We are glad that Farringford is ours.

Look over the inventory of the Seymour furniture & mark what we should like to have. Went on with *Troilus & Cressida* but A. says that he cannot read all to me. Our two little games of Backgammon.

May

2nd. We had a delightful time in the plantation and admired the Beech leaves coming out of their long brown tender spiral buds & the rich red brown sycamore leaves rising gracefully from their gorgeous crimson sheaths. In two or three other trees we have noticed the flowers coming out together with the leaves from the same sheath.

3rd. A. walks to Alum Bay. The water was low so that he could see the Bay from a greater distance than he had ever seen it before. He said that he had never seen it so fine. We see a field thick with white Narcissus.

4th. Thanksgiving for Peace—Go to Communion. Walk in the fields with the children who are much excited calling the birds to come & eat food that we have put for them under the Elm before the Drawing-room window. Poor little Hallam coloured with disappointment as they flew by unheedful of his call 'Come birdies it is very good'.

5th. Mr. Isaacson called & we subscribed to the church at Constantinople. I take the children to Captain Hamond's. We pass the rest of our neighbours on the road & so could not call. No neighbours could suit us better. All so kind & friendly & not expecting us to give great dinner parties or to join them. A. & I went to look at shells & chalk which Merwood had put for us in the Greenhouse & then to see if the potatoes he had planted were sprouting. I brought home a huge netting needle given me by Mrs. Hamond hoping that A. would learn to make nets for the garden as my Father does . . .

8th. He walks before breakfast & brings me flowers. Mr. Seymour asks thro' Mr. Sewell to have the house for packing. I begin separating books. A. reads me 'The Man of Law's Tale', Dame Custance,* which I admire extremely.

9th. A. walks before breakfast. He reads me 'The Monk's Tale' of the three men hunting Death to kill it. We have a little Backgammon afterwards, have been packing a little to-day.

10th. A. walks again before breakfast. Merwood comes to ask about making a private road for us to the Down. A. goes with him to look about it & then returns to take me out because it is so beautiful.

He goes to Swainston to meet the Monckton Milneses, I do not go because of the packing. A beautiful evening sad without him.

11th. Go to church, beautiful day. Sunset gorgeous colours of the rainbow on the shoulder of Afton down, distance lovely as can be.

12th. Mr. & Mrs. Monckton Milnes come with Sir John & Lady Simeon & A. to luncheon. A. took Mr. & Mrs. Milnes into the plantation. Sir John stayed behind to help me by taking down the books & then followed them & missed them. I had a pleasant talk with Lady Simeon. When our friends had gone we went all over the Farm buildings with Merwood even up the ladder into the granary.

13th. In the midst of all our confusion while all imaginable things strewed the drawing-room & the bookshelves were bare & the chairs & tables dancing, Prince Albert came. We wish things had instead been looking their best to have done him honour. One of the gentlemen with him gathered a great bunch of cowslips which the Prince admired very much & took them himself. One dropt & I kept it for the children as a memorial. A nightingale was singing while he was here I think. It had been singing delightfully all the morning close to the house. Afterwards A. & I had a very pleasant walk in the fields. He took me to that field where the great bunches of white Narcissus grow. The steep sand bank in it is very pretty. After dinner he came to fetch me that I might see the beautiful view from the North attic where he was sitting because his own was piled up with books & other things.

---

*From Geoffrey Chaucer's *Canterbury Tales.*

14th. After dinner we go to the Red House* which has since been Villa Doria, High Down Villa, Locksley. Mr. & Miss Seymour & a man servant arrive.

15th. Sir John Simeon, the Milneses, & Mr. Stephen de Vere called on their way to Alum Bay. We did not go. It rained so they had their luncheon at the Inn there & return for us. We go to Swainston.

16th. The Milneses leave. Sir John & Lady Simeon, Mr. de Vere, & ourselves go to Osborne. All except Mr. de Vere leave our names. The drive very pleasant. Mr. Wagy Prosser comes to dinner. Mr. de Vere plays some old Church music. Very beautiful.

17th. We return from our pleasant visit. We like our host & hostess more & more. We drive in an open carriage against a brisk west wind & enjoy it much. Soon after our arrival at our temporary home we have a message from Lambert telling us to expect the Queen, for orders for her reception had been given at Yarmouth and one of the carriages was to be in readiness to take HM to Freshwater Gate & the Prince had said to Captain F. on leaving Farringford, 'It is a pretty place, it is a pretty place. I shall certainly bring the Queen to see it'. We dressed our children in their rose-coloured dresses and all went into the Farringford garden to receive HM, not liking to go into the house tho' we did have rugs spread on the narrow path left between packages in the entrance hall. However, the Queen did not come probably because of the stormy morning. Edmund comes to dinner.

18th. A. & Edmund walk & admire a glorious bank of blue hyacinths waving in the wind.

19th. The Queen lays the foundation stone of the new Military Hospital so we do not expect her to-day. Mr. Palgrave & Mr. Sellar come to dinner. A little before A. & I had had a delightful walk which had led us in returning by the brook that runs thro' Sheepwash green. I praised its beauty to a man working in one of the cottage gardens. He said we do not think of it being near. I dare say it seems pretty to strangers. He told us that it was never dry.

20th. I spent my Louy's birthday partly in writing letters partly in expecting the Queen, for orders had again been received at Yarmouth.

21st. Captain Crozier told us that the Prince had put the cowslips

---

*The Red House was occupied by Tennysons for two weeks during renovations at Farringford.

in water meaning to make cowslip tea of them for the Queen & himself.

22nd. Miss Seymour goes.

23rd. Mr. Sellar leaves us. We like him exceedingly. Mr. Seymour calls to take leave & we hear that they are sorry to go.

24th. Mr. Palgrave goes. A. reads me part of the Review on Ruskin in the *Quarterly*.

26th. We go up to Farringford with Lambert to look at the furniture for which he is good enough to bid for us.

27th & 28th. Sale days. The week uncomfortable what with the sale & the children not being happy here.

29th. Go up to look at things and find a plain gold ring, a wedding ring we think, in a bed-room.

30th. The sweeps come. We look over our purchases with the auctioneer's clerk. Get to the Red House late for dinner. The evening splendid. Sunlight among the trees in the field seen thro' our kitchen garden beautiful. The ducks made a pleasant noise in that pleasant lane leading to our back gate. They sailed about snapping their bills catching some of the innumerable insects.

31st. Went to Communion, then to Farringford & rang at the front door as he told me & he opened it to me & we went about the house & garden.

June

1st. We began to unpack things & to take them into the house. Went back late to dinner. Weather most beautiful. We admire the view from the farm yard where the wall fringed with flowers and ivy over the garden gate is the foreground, where he had repeated to me that part of 'Enid' about the singing in the farm yard.

3rd. Unpacking again. Capt. & Mrs. Crozier bring Col. Ferber to see the rooms. Putting out beds on the grass. Splendid days.

4th. Unpacking still. We get the children's day nursery ready for them & I help E. to make Hallam's & Gandy's beds. We stay to welcome our children to their home. They run about delighted and Hallam asks, 'May I stay?' Then we go to dine at the Red House and come home by the garden. A beautiful evening. We stop at the barn &

look at Merwood's bits of carpet which he thought might do for us. I had sent to beg that he would not wait but there he sat in the barn his carpet spread out of doors. My A. gathered a rose and gave it to me as we walked thro' the kitchen garden. We went in at our back door. An evening to be remembered. A. gave me a welcome to our home which will be ever dear to memory. We had our tea in the drawing room. A. read me some of 'Enid'. It seemed as if we were the people of those old days. A Stag's horn beetle (I think it was) came into the room with a harp-like sound. We put it out & it sat on the window frame looking in at us & we admired its bright black eyes & its horns like the leaves of a Fan Palm, only they were brown yellow.

5th to 15th. Joiners mending many breakages. Great scrubbings going on, placing of furniture, hanging pictures, planning carpets, with occasional delight of glorious view of the Light-House glittering in the distance with laurels twinkling in the foreground under gloom of trees or of cliffs & sea gem-like.

15th. A. reads 'Griselda' to me, a favourite with me, and 'Enid' as far as it is done & we weed in the garden. He reads also some of Sidney Smith's life. Glad to see the great peonies we planted in the plantation growing.

18th. We go up the down, very beauitful & very delightful. Sain foin makes the hill crimson in a long slip. Pretty dwarf roses & great tracts golden with lady's fingers in other parts. We water & weed a little after rain.

21st. A pleasant walk in the fields. A. reads me a bit of Cambises. I am glad that we both like Chaucer so much.

22nd. Go to Church. A. reads me some of the epistle to the Romans. Baby runs in with two Bee orchises gathered near the Gate. I never saw any before & I am glad to see them. We admired the reflection of the clouds soft in the still sea. We saw a great ship pass majestically with troops from the Crimea & could not but think of the happy hearts that ship would make. How cold & blank the drawing room felt when I returned.

24th. All this week I bind manuscript books for A. & weed his potatoes and his 'clearing'.

27th. The Simeons come & like the house better with our furniture. They say it looks more homey. They go with me to the potatoes & the children bring Lady Simeon some tea.

Emily Tennyson, from the portrait at Aldworth, painted by G. F. Watts, R.A.

From the Tennyson Research Centre Collection, Lincoln, by courtesy of Lord Tennyson and Lincolnshire Library Service

The Tennyson Family, walking in the gardens of Farringford, May 1863, photographed by Rejlander

From the Tennyson Research Centre Collection, Lincoln, by courtesy of Lord Tennyson and Lincolnshire Library Service

July

2nd. A. arrives unexpectedly, brought news of a sad possibility respecting our affairs. He showed the noblest disregard of it much as the reality would affect us. I can never forget it. He admires the rooms.

3rd. We go into the withy bed to look for flowers. It is so much of a jungle we can scarcely get in & we are glad to find the willow herb we planted last year thriving under the fence. In the evening we went to look at the beautiful wild garden rose bush in the wilderness which made him think of Sunday mornings at Somersby when his Mother used always to gather a white rose.

4th. Charlie's birthday. A. & I went to watch Merwood's progress with the water-pipes. What beautiful white sand! Found the children playing in the chalk pit as we went up the down. Gandy at her crochet work. Built a castle for them & shot it down, gave them wild roses & returned home with them. Many wild flowers about & on the down the thyme is beautiful.

6th. Went to Communion & afterwards in the garden heard A.'s low whistle & found him lying by the strawberry bed under the trees nearest the wall. We walk in the fields. A beautiful day.

8th & 9th. Backgammon these nights. My birthday. Delightful letters from my Father & Louy, & from A. 'Why did you not tell me?' Better than a hundred letters had he written them.

10th. Mr. Peel comes. Mr. Bradley calls. Mr. & Mrs. Seymour call on their way to Chale. I promise to let them know if we let Farringford next year. The Bradleys come to Villa Doria (our Red House). Mr. Cotton calls. I busy planning a new Dairy. We receive a firefly which Mr. Smith has been so kind as to let Mr. Patmore send us. There are two raised lamps of yellow light behind its eyes, also a long slit in the body likewise bright with yellow light which we did not see at first until we had put in it water. We send it back by post. The children very pleased with it. The Bradleys send us a neck of Venison & dine with us.

11th. Mr. Bradley brings us his little basket carriage to look at. A meeting of the children. Little Arthur drives our Hallam & Lionel. The Bradleys & Mr. Peel dine with us.

12th. The beautiful contributions for the bazaar arrive from Grasby. The Bradleys in the evening. Edmund arrives at nearly twelve. All the servants gone to bed except Gandy who finds some cold lamb for Edmund. A. & I come down to him & Mr. Peel not knowing we are with him also comes down & kindly offers his room.

13th. A long talk with Edmund. Mr. Bradley calls. Sarah Hayward's most kind contributions to the bazaar.

14th. Mr. Peel & Edmund go at 7 in the morning. I busy in making an Inventory of all the things in the house. We discover a great well of water in the cellar which must be drained away as we never mean to use the hot water apparatus running thro' two floors of the house. Drains bad as they have never been before. Bradleys in the evenings.

15th. Inventory again. A. persuades me to go up the down with him. Air warm, down very sweet, flowers beautiful, centaury just coming out. Mr. Bradley calls. I sent off my Bazaar things to Lady Worsley Holmes.

September

26th. On our way from Gloucester we pass encampments and barrows on the downs and reach Salisbury. How pure & beautiful the Cathedral & how striking the tombs between each pair of pillars. It was the Friday afternoon service and we heared 'He was despised' sung. Very affecting to both of us. We meant to have taken Gandy & the children next morning but it was a pouring rain. It cleared however a little before we started and we have a delightful passage, quick & sunny, and a bright drive home. Both the children very merry. Hallam exclaims, there is Farringford, as he comes to the bell & is very excited at getting home. How cheerful & airy & beautiful home looks!

28th. Hallam will not believe it is Sunday because it rains. For our Welsh we only read the Hundredth psalm to-day.

29th. How gem-like the beauty of our view towards Blackgang looks. We make out a little of 'Enid' in Welsh & in the evening I play some Welsh airs & A. reads as much of his 'Enid' as is sufficiently finished.

30th. We go up the Down. A. reads me the beginning of *Troilus & Cressida.*

October

1st. Mr. Moxon comes for a few hours. Very kind about advancing us money. A. goes with him as far as he goes on the way to Swainston.

The road not yet done.

2nd. A. cannot return to-day as he had intended because of the rain.

3rd. He walks home to-day. We look at the little American edition which is very pretty.

5th. After Communion sit in the Arbour with A. & he walks on the down at night. The stars are splendid. He talks with the coast guard who says how much happier the French sailors are than ours. I hope it is not so. Our new post-bag looks like home.

6th. Every day A. walks with me about the garden & the fields.

7th. (I think it is) We get Mr. Lee's kind note & *The Lives of the British Saints* and what he has copied about King Arthur—26 or 27 pages of copy book.

8th. So much letter-writing that some days I have no time even for a little Welsh Bible.

10th. Very fine. I take a holiday from letter-writing & have a ride in the Rocking-Chair in the garden while A. clears out Quitch [couch grass].

11th. Quitch again tho' it is rainy & misty. I get A. to read me a good part of 'Maud' before it goes for a second edition. Merwood in trouble about the sheep the dog has worried on the down and the court martial. A. reads me a bit of 'Enid'.

13th. 14th. A bit of 'Enid' these two evenings.

15th. Mr. & Mrs. Patmore cross in an open boat. Rash the landlord says in the storm.

16th. A luncheon party of fifteen to meet Mr. & Mrs. Albert Hamburgh. The A. Court Holmeses, Simeons, Capt. & Mrs. Hamond, . . . Mr. Cornwall Simeon, Mr. & Mrs. Clough. Everybody very kind.

17th. A. with his Quitch again. The Cloughs come to dinner. Very taking they are.

18th. 'Enid' in the evening. The Patmores delighted.

21st. 'Merlin'. The Patmores think it still grander. They are so kind. They take long walks in the morning that I may not be tired.

22nd. We hear from Park House that dear little Eddy was taken from them on the 20th. A boy of great promise & Edmund's only Son. Very sad.

23rd. The Patmores go to Swainston. I like them more and more.

24th, 25th, 26th, 27th. Isaiah one evening & Chaucer the other evenings. Walking & sweeping leaves. Very pleasant days.

29th. Mr. Dempster arrives in the evening having been grounded two hours the hawsers having broken. He sings 'The May Queen' to us.

30th. Walks with A. in the morning to the Needles and sings to the children & in the evening to us.

31st. Miss Cotton & Miss Southwell come to hear Mr. Dempster sing in the evening. The Simeons call. A. walks on Afton Down in the morning.

November

1st. A. walks with Mr. Dempster to the Ferry. Chaucer.

3rd. The Simeons in the evening. Very pleasant evening.

4th. Beautiful day again, walking, sweeping leaves, & Chaucer.

5th. We hear that we have lost only 200 in the Ding Bank troubles. We feared that it might have been much worse & we are glad & thankful. A. has put down all 'Enid' to read to me & reads it this evening. These delightful walks & readings do me a great deal of good.

6th. Very indifferent news of my dear Father. A. very good to me. He reads me the alterations in 'Enid'. The big screens he has put up for me in the drawing room amuse the children very much. Baby says he is going up a mountain.

8th. Send the photographs of A.'s medallion & mine to my Father for his birthday.

11th. 'Enid'.

12th. 'Merlin'.

13th. Dr. Mann shows his microscope to Merwood & to us. The butterfly's tongue a coiled bracelet of filagree gold, the silk worm's spiracle, a splinter of Fir wood & one of Mahogany. All wonderful & beautiful.

14th. A. & I set off for Park House. The short angry white waves rather alarm one. The spray makes us wet at first but the boat goes smoothly. The sun is bright but the wind cold. My A. protects me from it with numberless cloaks & wrappers. We dine at Somerset House & Poor Edmund meets us at the train & dines there too.

15th. To the Dentist & then to Park House.

16th. We talk about different things and about Eddy. The place looks splendid with the autumn leaves in the sunshine.

17th. 'Enid' to-night after a day of talking.

18th. We go to see Tom Lushingtons at the Stacey House. They come to dinner.

20th. Dentist, Aunt Franklin, Sophy Cracroft, LeFroys, Mr. Woolner, Mr. Palgrave, L. Simpkinson, Mr. Buchanan. Read in the evening. A. buys Physical Atlas & other books & hears people asking for Tennyson's poems for prizes, gives the name of Weld for his purchases.

21st. We return home, leave London in a fog but find only a light mist with gray clouds in the country. The children's joyful greeting 'I am very glad to see you' as they run & skip with beaming eyes very delightful. Dr. Mann reports the progress of drains & stoves which he has been so good as to superintend for us. The children very pleased with the numbers of Schnorr's Bible which we brought them, Grandpapa's gift.

27th. 'Aurora Leigh' from Mr. Browning.

December

3rd. A letter to say that all is settled about Farringford. A letter misses the owner, changes the place of payment, so all these days we have been anxious & now we are glad & thankful that the place is our own. Today Mr. Isaacson calls & talks a long while about troubles in the Parish which troubles us. A. remarks to me on the news coming as it does on the day we have heard that Farringford is our own. I finish 'Aurora Leigh' today. I go out & find A. at the Leaf heap which he has kept up very diligently these days that I might not smell the drain work which has been going on. He reads to me the first part of *Julius Caesar*. The boys very happy getting jogged both together on his knees.

4th. A letter from poor Mother. Very cheerful but telling us that one eye fails.

6th. These days reading Johnston's *Agricultural Chemistry* & Vilemarque's *Bardes Bretons.*

7th. Communion. Two wrecks of Fruit Vessels & two poor men drowned.

9th. See to the planting of crocuses. mezereon, Lilacs which came yesterday & to the building of a stove in the Greenhouse. A. rolls the grass by moonlight & goes to the sea. Stormy.

10th. Stormy again but Mrs. Cameron's good Ellen comes with Arnoll's fittings for the drawing room fireplace notwithstanding.

11th. A. dines with Captain Crozier and meets Capt. & Mrs. Fenwick, Miss Jean Murdoch, Capt. & Mrs. Hamond & has a very pleasant evening. A great thunder storm. While he is away his books in the new shelves—the Welsh shelves & others. He is surprised to find them done.

12th & 13th. Stormy still. A. rolls the grass.

15th. Sir John Simeon comes to lunch & to hear 'Enid'. The Arnoll brick stove in the Greenhouse lighted for the first time. It answers very well.

16th. Plumbers, Glaziers, Carpenters, Bricklayers, a fearful array of workmen. We get the Greenhouse made tidier. The Barometer has taken a most wonderful leap of about a quarter of a circle in one day & of half the circle in two or three days.

17th. We hear of Horatio's engagement to Charlotte Elwes.

18th. Mr. Palgrave arrives unexpectedly and comes laden with books, a welcome sight to us. I perceive the beginnings of baby's illness.

20th. A. reads half 'Enid'.

21st. Mr. Henry Smith calls while I am with poor baby. I send word that A. is on the down. He finds him & Mr. Palgrave & comes in the evening with Miss Price. They are very kind & agreeable.

22nd. A. goes to the Coal-meeting at the Rectory, finishes 'Enid' in the evening. Mr. Palgrave delighted.

23rd. We persuade Mr. Palgrave to stay. A. reads a little Milton.

24th. Mr. Palgrave goes, a beautiful day he has, we are sorry he is going. Afton party call. Captain & Mrs. Hamond come. The Capt. brings a Turkish pipe for A. and they kindly press me to go with him to the Jubilee on the 30th. Were things otherwise I should like to go but of course I cannot leave baby.

25th. A. & I alone. We have a grand Yule log & our baby is rather better. Dr. Mann's powder sent in a letter has done him good. A.

digs diligently & rolls & reads 'La Petite Fadette' & the first book of *Paradise Regained.* To the children he says 'Ye Mariners of England' & they repeat it with great glee.

30th. He goes to the Hamond Jubilee & takes Mr. Stokes, In spite of the beautiful white gloves with which I provide him & which he wears, he does not dance. He talks to Sir Graham of Nelson. Sir Graham shows A. his portrait & promises to show him a Panorama of the battle of Copenhagen. He takes Mrs. Grosvenor Hood to supper. Every one very kind & friendly. Mr. Stokes gives him one of his Garland bits for the children.

31st. We were to have gone to Swainston for the Christmas tree to-morrow but can not because of baby tho' he is much better. He reads me The Spanish Armada & we look at Wilmot's book together.

1857

January

1st. A beautiful day. A. reads me some of Shakespeare's Sonnets & other things. Baby out a little to-day & has meat again.

2nd. Sir John Simeon & Mr. Pollen lunch with us, admire our boys, & the illustrations to his poems. He reads some Burns to me.

A. rolls diligently. Groves gives up his keys. Merwood enters in the farm cottage.

6th. A. reads to me some of the seven poems hung up in the Temple of Mecca & tells me that these were the true inspiration of 'Locksley Hall'. He wonders that he has never read them to me before & told me this. 2nd and 3rd Books of *Paradise Regained.* The Haunch of Venison. Gray's 'Eton'. He rolls in the daytime.

10th. Mr. Archibald Peel comes. He & A. go up the down at night. I see a white owl in the Ilex.

11th. We go to Church & they go down to the sea at night after A. has read the 4th book of *Paradise Regained.*

12th. Sir John Simeon & his brother Cornwall come to dinner. We have a pleasant evening. I see some snowdrops.

13th. Some of the Afton party in the evening. Ghost stories, 'The Tapestried Chamber' & others.

14th & 15th. Shakespeare's 'Let me not'. A little 'Maud' & a great deal of talk.

16th. 'Maud'. I leave before the sad part.

17th. Mr. Peel rushes suddenly to Chester. I write letters to know what chance he would have for Newport. Capt. Hamond kindly calls to talk to me & say he is too late. A. walks to Swainston to meet one of the candidates & his friend Mr. Beaumont. I send forward his portmanteau that he may go on to Bonchurch for he has not been well these last days & I think he wants change. I look after the garden walks & the little gate into 'The Wife's Walk' for A.

21st. A letter from Sir John saying that A. will return to-day. Lady Simeon, Miss Simeon, & Mr. Bonham Carter bring him. He sees the gate & approves.

22nd. We look after the workmen, & he reads me some of *Hamlet* in the evening.

23rd. Workmen, rolling, & some Richard III.

24th. Workmen again, some Henry VI.

25th. The 55th Chapter of Isaiah. Too stormy for Church.

Swainston Manor

26th. We walk a little in the Wife's walk. He prunes apple trees. He reads me some of *Timon.*

Hamonds, Croziers, Afton party all very kind in coming to see us. No formality of calls returned. They know I have too much to do to pay visits often. Walks about the fields these days. The land seems much impoverished. A. reads some of Garth Wilkinson on Egypt to me. Review of Swedenborg in the February *Fraser* which A. reads to me.

February

1st. Go to Communion & hear a bird sing while waiting at the Church door more sweetly than almost any I ever heard. A wood Lark, I think. A. reads Swedenborg's *Heaven & Hell.*

3rd. A. begins to translate the *Prometheus Bound* of Aeschylus to me.

4th. He burns leaves in Maiden's Croft as he did yesterday and he gets me the long bench to lie down upon & gives me his cloak. Smoke & flames very beautiful when Merwood put in the Brambles. Little feathery tongues of flame. Most beautiful day A. reads me part of an Essay from the *Quarterly* of October on Physionomy [*sic*].

5th. We go out to the field with cinders & lime and send for soot-lime. We have a long talk with Merwood on farming matters. A. draws me in Mr. Bradley's little carriage with a view of buying it. I am reading the last volume of Lord Mahon which interests me extremely. A. reads to me of Fergusson's *Architecture.* Mr. & Mrs. Lewis call.

6th. A. drives me in Mr. Bradley's carriage to see whether it will do for us. It shakes too much unfortunately. Mr. & Mrs. Lewis come in the evening.

7th. We spread ashes just outside the iron fence & then go into the Avenue field & consent to the cutting down of three small Elms in the way of the Plough. A. sees Merwood feed his sheep & talks to him about the Moon. I finish Lord Mahon, sorry that it is come to an end.

9th & 10th. We look after workmen & A. reads *Macbeth* to me.

11th. We pour quicklime & put cinders under the Chestnut trees in the Park. The green moss turns a beautiful red.

12th. See an elm hauled down with a rope. [Read] a little of a gardening book at night. A thrush sings as if mad with delight.

13th. The children delighted with the help they think they give in hauling down trees. We see Jupiter & Venus near each other. A splendid sight. The days have been beautiful, frost at night but sunny days not cold.

Lady Simeon calls to look after us. Very kind she is. A. reads all Milton's Sonnets to me & some of Cicero on Immortality.

Backgammon, A. not being well enough to read.

17th. Mrs. Charles West & her sister Charlie come all the way from

St. Laurence's cottage to breakfast. Walk to the beacon with A. & return after tea. A. goes with me to find the lost seat of my stool.

Walks in the fields & gardens & on the down. Birds sing delightfully, the sea mews cry. A. puts his cloak over me that I may see Jupiter from his study window. He sees him from the room silvering a cloud. A. reads to me the reign of John in Sharon Turner, some of Burton's *Anatomy of Melancholy* in the evenings.

21st. Mrs. Cameron comes with Charlie & Henry, plays pelican* for the boys. A. makes the path up to Maiden's Croft.

22nd. & shows Mr. & Mrs. Cameron the wilderness & Maiden's Croft & garden & farm yard.

23rd. Mr. Estcourt & Woodford come to look over the Farm & to settle things & Sir John in the kindness of his heart rides over to see if he can help. Mr. & Mrs. Cameron, Julia, & Mr. Charles Henry Cameron dine with us. The Afton ladies in the evening.

24th. Welcome the old almost bedridden mother to the farmhouse who is much tired by the removal. Doomed dead trees which must be cut down, and lament the big Pine at the gate.

25th. A. brings me violets & primroses at breakfast time. The pretty little basket carriage which Mr. Archibald Peel has kindly chosen for us arrives. Mr. C. H. Cameron leaves. We begin our half-past six o'clock dinner. Hitherto we have dined at five or half-past & our friends say have kept our clocks half an hour too fast. Very likely. There is no very exact record of time here. A. works till one generally when we lunch & as soon as they are old enough our boys dine with us. A. walks & works out of doors with me & when they are old enough we have them with us in the afternoon. He reads me some of Speddings's *Bacon.* Delightful to me.

26th. Carts of seaweed on the Park. The Simeons & Camerons to dinner.

27th. The children a pretty happy sight in the wilderness. Hardinge leading Lionel by the hand, Hallam leading all. Then they come each with a bunch of snowdrops or primroses. Hallam runs with his rosy cheeks to kiss me then I have a kiss from all.

28th. Mr. & Mrs. Cameron & Julia come to tea that they may hear 'Enid'.

---

*Pelican – card game.

March

1st. After Communion A. & I walk in the fields & then call on the Merwoods & taste her Currant & greengage wines.

A blackbird sings with something of the sweet sad note of that which charmed me at Hale. I think I never heard another like it. The thrushes mad with joy. There is a continual ripple of song either from starlings or redwings. Daily meetings with the Camerons.

2nd. 'Merlin' read.

3rd. I promised to go with A. & them to Swainston if it were fine. It was misty & I did not go.

4th. Mr. Cameron & Julia find us marking Maiden's Croft as we do these days, A. & Me.

6th. Mr. Cameron dines & they plan a visit to Bonchurch & A. wants me to go but it seems more prudent that I should stay at home. I write many letters after having turned the clay a little in Maiden's Croft & Pathacre as A. bid me.

9th. A. returns late. I amuse myself with my Piano waiting for him.

10th. A. takes Julia & Hardinge to the Meet at Afton. Her Mother is in bed & a mistake about the carriage for me & we do not like to disappoint Julia. I hear the first dove. Mrs. Cameron comes to dinner.

11th. We at our church again. A. reads some of *The Wisdom of Solomon* [one of the books of the *Apocrypha*] to me & tells me the passages he marked when reading it to Arthur Hallam.

12th. In the fields again. Mr. Warburton comes while we are at dinner & stays with us. Mrs. Cameron in the evening. Mr. Warburton leaves next morning. Mrs. Cameron in the evening.

14th. We in Pathacre spreading earth & lime when Mr. Cameron comes to walk. It is so windy. A. soon tired of walking, comes again with him to Pathacre. He thinks it too windy for me to stay & finished the work alone. Mr. Cameron has gone to fetch Mr. Prinsep who has brought a hundred violet roots for us. A. goes to the sea which has been rolling with a grand continuous roll. Hallam asks if Mr. Prinsep will have an ugly nose again. I puzzle for a moment & remember the naughty Princess of the Fairy story. The flower of the wood laurel beautiful now. A. reads to me a little Milton.

15th. Mrs. Cameron, Mrs. Prinsep, Julia & Alice to nursery tea.

A. reads me more chapters of *The Wisdom of Solomon.*

16th. Sir John & Lady Simeon come to luncheon & bring Johnnie to meet the little Camerons at Lionel's birthday dinner. Mrs. Cameron, Hardinge, & Alice come afterwards with a fire balloon & little lamps of Noah's Ark flags & such things. They find us in Hill Close breaking chalk & they come trooping back with all the children. The fire balloon catches fire while the gentlemen are racing with the children. Mrs. Cameron & Ellen deck the furze bush with toys & lamps & we draw lots. I so tired that A. will not have anyone in the evening. Our guests depart after five o'clock tea. The calm of nights beautiful. These days work again in the fields. The gulls make a wild noise every day now. Mrs. Cameron & Mrs. Prinsep to dinner or in the evenings. I receive Froude's *England* from Mr. Warburton—a most welcome gift.

23rd. We dine with the Camerons after our usual field work. Mrs. Cameron gives me Henry Taylor's poems beautifully bound in crimson. Hardinge brings me home. A. stays & reads the scene from *Pericles.* I finish copying 'Enid'.

24th. The Camerons go to Swainston & come for 'Merlin' in the even.

25th. A. reads to me some of Froude.* Very pleasant to me. The first lark to-day, I think. Merwood finds a bat sleeping in an old Ash tree which he cuts down in the Rue. He brings it into the drawing room & it awoke & flies about but at last it is caught & put out of the window. We cut down a dead Acacia for A.'s desk.

26th. He works always in the fields & I look on. We talk this evening & he goes late to the Camerons & finds four military men there. They had all been dragging the Bay & he brings a basket of Fish home with him. Holland had gone to bed & hears him pumping for he had found a tub & had put the fish in & was pumping over them.

27th. Sir John & Mr. & Mrs. Cameron dine. Mrs. Prinsep in the evening. Sorry that she is going. Next morning Sir John leaves & A. walks with him to the hotel taking R. Doyle's picture of the view from Farringford & Miss Sewell's Lake Tennyson in New Zealand, so named by Mr. Frederic Weld, to be framed. Eleanor West and Horatio arrive.

31st. Sir John comes from the nomination to dine here in April. He canvasses. Mr. Wood calls and dines with us . . .

---

*James Anthony Froude (1818-94) published *History of England,* etc. (1856-70).

April

1st. A. reads some of the paper on Rats in the *Quarterly.* It makes one feel an affection for them, telling how they lead about & take care of the blind & how they have attached themselves to man. It also tells how the old British rat, being weaker than the Hanoverian, it fights in companies whenever it can.

3rd. Polling day here. The grass looks very rich where we have put the clay & Merwood the seaweed. Horatio and Eleanor go.

6th. I send off the last proof sheets of the Illustrated Edition. We put the cuttings of our hair & the children's in the ground round the cabbage roses. Look at the livestock on the farm with Merwood & tell him that the importation of Cattle from certain parts is forbidden because of murrain [infectious disease in cattle].

9th. We hear the first nightingale. A. reads me a little Froude in the evening.

10th. He goes on the Down & talks to the coast guard about Jesus Christ as we had been talking before he went out. 'A great day to-day' (Good Friday), the coast guard began, & they talked on.

11th. Mrs. Cameron comes with Mr. Steven & lunches.

13th. Eleanor West takes the Red Cottage.

14th. Captain & Mrs. Hamond dine with us. Julia & Mrs. Prinsep & the Afton young ladies in the evening.

15th. We go to St. Laurence for Horatio's wedding. The day beautiful, a delightful drive. Banks flowery with primroses circle the fine wall of the Undercliff which as A. says looks as if some old order of architecture, knolls gorgeous with furze backed by the sea. We went into the garden of the Black Gang Hotel. I looked down the path which Papa & I descended some twelve years ago. We think the garden of the St. Laurence Cottages a Paradise which had been lent to Charles by his cousin. Knolls of greenest, smoothest turf & primrose banks & walks, trees, a rocky stream, splendid flowers in beds & the sea for background. They kindly make me lie down in the drawing room & have my dinner there. A package comes from Mr. Peel. A. and Dudley unpack it in the midst of sundry, laughing conjectures . . . A. & I go to the Pelham Cottage. The stars are bright & the rooks cawing at eleven o'clock. We stumble about for it is too dark to see the paths but make our way to the light in the house at last.

16th. Stormy clouds but only two little showers during the day & a good deal of sunshine. The little church gay with hothouse & greenhouse flowers. Charlie looks very pretty in her wreath & veil a Horatio his very best. A pleasure to see their happy faces. The rooms & the breakfast table decked with primroses. All very cheerful. After breakfast we all dance under the Verandah. A. & I arm in arm. We throw a large horseshoe once belonging to a Lincolnshire cart-horse & our oldest old slipper after them for good luck. About three when the bride & bridegroom have left for Winchester, A. & I & Mrs. West drive to Bonchurch to call on Manns, Peels & Whites, the rest ride on horseback. Mr. Hamburgh, the Miss Sewells & their friend Miss Frederick, & Mr. Field's friend Mr. Latham, & Dr. Mann dine. A. does the honours, Dudley not being well enough. I sit near A. at dinner to my delight.

17th. He walks with Eleanor to see the Pillar named after A. by Dr. Kane of which Miss Sewell is so very [bold] as to make a water-colour drawing for us. After luncheon we return home. Another charming drive and a delightful welcome from the boys who come skipping downstairs singing in chorus, 'I am so glad you're come home, I'm so glad you're come home', & to see how Hallam plays the host to us. We unpack the frigate which Mr. Peel has sent us to the joy of the children.

18th. Mrs. Cameron & Julia to tea with Mrs. Prinsep. We hear that Mr. Southey has been photographing the children.

19th. Ladies in the evening.

20th. They go today. We are sorry. Dr. & Mrs. Vaughan come. A. reads a great part of Job to me.

22nd. A. mows. Mr. Arthur Stanley comes, goes up the down with A., dines & sleeps. Dessert in the drawing room. A very pleasant talk & a little bit of 'Maud'. Mr. Stanley never likes visiting the same place twice—Waste of time—or does not like disturbing 1st impressions.

23rd. Mr. Stanley goes after I have had a very pleasant talk with him. We cannot but be sorry that he must go.

24th. A beautiful Thomas à Kempis sent me by Sir John as an Easter gift.

Woodford comes & we go about the Farm with him. A. reads me some of Colomba. Mr. Reginald Southey's photograph of the boys arrives. One can trace some likeness to Hallam in that of Hallam little ruffian tho' he be. Lionel comes out still less distinctly but one is grateful. We look after the gates with Merwood. A. reads me some of Agatha and Cecile.

26th. A little bit of 'Merlin'.

27th. A. goes to London. Only a little open carriage comes for us. I say I fear that there is no room for you, my children. Poor Hallam's eyes fill with tears so we each take a child on our knees. Rather late for the steamer but A. rows after it and it stops & he gets on board. The dentist detains him longer than we expected. I look after calves, poultry, & vine, plant roses & clematis & woodbine near his chair in the corner of the kitchen garden (I call it his but he put it there for me), & one rose tree near our arbour, tie up lettuces for him, put pine branches in the hedge near where it is thin, get lilies of the valley for his room, write many letters, & read a little. His gold pear comes.

May

6th. His Acacia wood desk which I have had made for him out of one of our own Acacias comes & I write a letter to him on it.

Hallam writes his own letter to Papa to-day, 13th.

15th, 16th, 17th. A. writes every day but I am made sad. Some days by the negligence of the post office my letters coming two together instead of one every day. My days all much the same.

18th. He comes home to-day with Mr. Woolner & Mr. Vernon Lushington. The photograph priceless (Cundall's), so much the best I have seen.

19th. A delightful & very happy walk. The wilderness a paradise of flowers—blue hyacinths like the Heavens breaking thro' the earth, orchises, gorgeous crimson crown in the Pine trees. A. covered with sweet golden dust from them. The cedar brightening with the new leaves. A. read the 'Ode to the Duke of Wellington' in the evening & told Mr. Lushington the song from 'Merlin'.

20th. Horatio, Mr. Worsley, Mr. Wise & Dudley Elwes come in a boat & had to return at once because of the tide & so did not see A. who had gone with the two gentlemen to Alum Bay. He reads 'Maud'.

21st. They walk towards Compton Bay & he reads *Hamlet*.

22nd. Mr. Lushington brings me Rock-roses from the Cliff. Sun roses they are called because they open at sunrise & the petals fall at sunset. He & Mr. Woolner have a beautiful walk to Cliff End & admire the views from the lane leading to it. A. reads 'Audley Court' & other things. Mrs. Cameron sends me the Portfolio with Mr. Southey's photograph of the boys.

23rd. Mr. Lushington & Mr. Woolner go, with a hope on our part that they may come again before long. Mr. Wilberforce comes.

24th. All go to Church. A. reads Milton.

25th. Milton.

27th. We admire the golden leaves of the Black Poplar bright with sunshine against the dark Fir trees.

28th. Mr. Wilberforce goes. Mother & Matilda come. A great deal of writing all these days.

June

1st. We send off 'Enid' to Moxon!

3rd. Mr. & Mrs. Archibald Peel dine with us. Borton is here.

10th. I get up early to see dear Gandy off, obliged to send her away for fear of bad effects on our Hallam from favouritism to Lionel whom she had from the first. Dreary days of discomfort & sadness from parting.

11th. Mr. & Mrs. Peel walk to Alum Bay & The Needles with A. and dine with us.

12th. Sir John & Captain Simeon call. We walk & talk and are very glad to have them back again. A. resolves not to publish 'Nimuë' ('Vivien') & 'Enid' until he has a bigger book.

13th. We take the children for a walk in honour of our wedding day.

15th. Stormy East winds. Poor A.'s Hayfever very bad. He had scarcely anything of it last year.

17th. Horatio & Charlie come.

19th. Edmund & Cissy. Drives to Norton, Totland Bay, Needles, Alum Bay, Brook, Mr. Bayard Taylor comes. We are all sorry that he only stays one night.

29th. The Bradleys come & Miss Price. Edmund & Cissy go.

30th. Arthur Wright comes.

Farringford House, Freshwater

From the Tennyson Research Centre Collection, Lincoln, by courtesy of Lord Tennyson and Lincolnshire Library Service

The Poet's Study, Farringford House

From the Tennyson Research Centre Collection, Lincoln, by courtesy of Lord Tennyson and Lincolnshire Library Service

Farringford today: now a hotel *photo R.J.H.*

July

1st. The Bradleys, Mr. Conington, Mr. Ellis and their two friends come in the evening.

2nd. Horatio & Arthur go in a boat to the Needles. Bring home a gull & two guillemots (willies).

3rd. Arthur goes. Mr. Reginald Cholmeley calls among others.

4th. Mr. Lear comes.

6th. Sir John & Lady Simeon dine here & Mr. George Coltman who is staying here. The Bradleys & Miss Price, the Afton party & Mr. Ellis & Mr. Rutsan. All charmed with Mr. Lear's singing.

7th. Mr. Coltman goes before we are up. We are touched by hearing him creep softly down stairs. Mr. Lear goes after having sung all the morning. Lionel throws himself on my knee & seems quite overpowered by music.

8th. An Italian sings to a kind of lyre.

9th. All our guests go. The first evening we have been alone for two months or more. A. busy examining the snakes' eggs which Merwood brought in yesterday having found them buried two or three feet down.

The snake hearts beat at least two hours after having been taken in the thin jelly sheath out of the leathery egg. A. puts my cloaks & cushions by the myrtle under the cedar tree & I lie down. The view splendid. He brings me the first lines which may be the nucleus of the parting of Arthur & Guinevere.

12th. We go with our children into the Hay field. The children very merry out with us. I have a very nice talk with A. in the evening.

13th. Hay field. The Bradleys, Miss Price & Mr. O'Grady to tea.

14th. Splendid weather. A. drives with Mr. Bradley to Heathfield & then waters Nemophila & puts out Lilies of the Valley. Mr. Bradley in the evening. A pleasant talk after A. had read me some of Shakespeare's Sonnets.

15th. Mr. Bradley helps me to arrange the books before we leave home. He very kind. I working till one or two o'clock in the morning.

16th. Mr. Bradley comes to help & to say good-bye. We have a prosperous journey & go to Draper's Hotel. We go to Burlington House. A. sleeps there & dines.

17th. Burlington House & Cudall's to have the children photographed. We go to Little Holland House & are charmed with the House & gardens. Mr. Prinsep most kind. I am introduced to Mr. Prinsep & both A. & I to Mr. Watts and Mr. Traherne. Then we go to Argyll Lodge. No one at home . . .

[The Tennyson's journey north, stopping to visit Bayons Manor and the Mausoleum at Brocklesby, where Hallam 'wants to call to the Dead. He says there are giants there'. At Manchester, Alfred is particularly pleased by Turner's sketches and Gainsborough's portrait of the 'Blue Boy'; on a more contemporary note, they hear Charles Dickens read his 'Christmas Carol' at the Free Trade Hall. Reaching the Lake District, they visit Furness Abbey and Langdale Pikes, as well as meeting Charles Dodgson – who photographed them – for the first time. Continuing their progress northwards into Scotland, 'A. is taken out in the boat dredging & is much interested by the curious beasties found'. Back in London, Alfred reads 'Morte d'Arthur' and 'Break, Break' to a company which includes Dante Rossetti and Holman Hunt.]

November

4th. Still we joyfully return, for all the enjoyment we have had, to our own darling home. Day rainy at first. Mrs. Cameron runs after us and comes with us [from London]. Clear as we cross. Rosy streaks as we near home at sunset. The children lavish all manner of tender words on their home. A. reads me some Dante—the Francesca, Ugolino, Daniella, Farinata, Cavelcanti.

5th. We write letters & go into Maiden's Croft & the garden. We find golden egg-like things on two sets of plants. These days about home & sweeping leaves after our old fashion. Our friends call.

10th. A little Lucretius.

11th. Odes of Gray, Coleridge & Shelley, Very delightful.

12th. Some Livingstone.

16th. Sweep leaves too late & get cold. A. reads me some of Grove's Correlations.

19th. Some of Béranger's Songs.* Lucretius & Béranger. I go on with Livingstone to myself.

---

*P. J. de Béranger (1780-1857); French poet.

21st. A. works very hard in the garden all these days. My cold too bad to go out. A. reads me some of Harry Lushington's things. 'La Nation Boutiquière', 'Inhermann' & we agree that they are very noble. How much we do miss him.

30th. A. reads me part of *Much Ado about Nothing,* rather in memory of Augustus Stafford whom he saw act Benedick in their college days, I think.

December

1st. Sir John & his brother Cornwall Simeon call. More of *Much Ado* in the evening.

2nd. A. reads me 'Sea Dreams'. Very fine, I think.

3rd. A. walks to the Simeons, returns on the 4th. He makes an old woman for them with his hand & then I kissed them sitting with Papa on the floor to their great delight.

8th. Sir John fetches him to Swainston. Hallam whispering over and over again in Sir John's hearing, 'Why does he go?' He returns next day, reads to me some of Jocelyn two or three evenings but we cannot get on with it. Sir Alexander Grant's book pleases me very much. A little *Hamlet* & 'Comus'.

19th. A lovely day. Mr. Palgrave comes. He comes always laden like Schiller's Lady from the Strange land. The children delighted with the pictures of the Fairy Tales and bon bon voices [?] which he has kindly brought them. A. works the garden as usual and walks with me when I can walk.

23rd. Sir John dines with us.

24th. A. brings me a nosegay of white wild roses & tells me that there are plenty more in the hedge, also bramble flowers and a little bit of woodbine but this is rather withered. The holly wreaths just up. A. reads 'Griselda' to us. A delightful evening.

25th. A beautiful sunny day. Went to Communion. A letter from Colonel Phipps asking by desire of the Queen that A. would write a stanza to 'God Save the Queen' to be sung at a concert which is to be given at Buckingham Palace on the evening of the Princess Royal's wedding day.

A. reads some of Rogers to us.

28th. Mr. Palgrave goes. We resolve after all to fight our way thro' Jocelyn.

30th. A letter from Colonel Phipps approving, I hope, of the two stanzas sent on the 27th. A. & I walk & sweep up leaves & burn them as usual.

1858

January

1st. Thankful indeed ought we to be that we begin the New Year as the old was ended in our happy daily round of work indoors & out or in pleasant walks when outdoors work could not be.

2nd. We decide on putting the little gate at the end of the Wilderness & we do finish Jocelyn.

3rd. A. reads me the histories of Jeptha & of Samson.

4th & 5th. Morte d'Arthur. Invitation to the Concert at Buckingham Palace. The Somersby pictures come. Every evening we act fairy tales & nursery stories for the boys, being Mother Hubbard or her dog or the Frog Prince or the Bird & Mouse or even Sausage as may be.

7th. Finish hanging the Somersby pictures. The boys find a little robin dead but still warm & Lionel kisses it over & over & makes me kiss it, & Hallam & A. make a grave for it in Hallam's garden between the Alexandrian laurel & the Russian violets & Lionel puts it in. They have made me carry it part of the way. A. tells them to say 'God bless you' to it & we put some of the feathers which have fallen off into Lionel's garden. A. reads me the end of the *Morte d'Arthur.* It is awe-inspiring.

The legend of the *Giant's Horseman*—his horse is bridled by the Arctic Circle—seems to me very fine.

8th. He reads to me the beginning of his parting of King Arthur & Guinevere. Grand and gigantic almost awe-inspiring some of it seems to me.

9th. When the boys & I have done our 'Plays', A. comes & reads their favourite nursery rhymes—Fox, My Lady Lea & the Three Huntsmen. He reads me the greater part of the History of Saul in 'Samuel'. Next evening Saul & David.

12th. We look about a site for the Summer House. Mr. Swinburne & his friend Mr. Hatch come & dine here. A. reads 'Maud' & when I am gone upstairs, King Arthur's speech.

15th. A. goes on with 'Kings' & reads me more of his 'Arthur & Guinevere', to my mind the grandest thing he has ever done & what he reads more beautifully if possible than anything else. He sends the hundred copies of the Stanzas to Colonel Phipps for the Queen.

17th. He reads me Guinevere's speech. Four days he walks to the Needles & other days long walks.

21st. He comes into the Nursery & reads 'The Sultan' to the children, also their favourite 'Snow White & Rose Red', then 'Briar Rose'.

22nd. He finishes 'Kings' to me which he has been reading almost every evening.

25th. Princess Royal's wedding day. I was telling Hallam what twins meant saying that they came into the world together, that he came alone, that Lionel did, that I did, upon which he indignantly replied, he, not you, you came down from Heaven with Papa.

A. makes the boys very happy by building a city for Hallam & defending while Hallam fires.

February

1st. Cities built again & again by the boys & A. He looks to the building of our Summer House & reads me in the evening Juvenal's 13th Satire in Latin & then translates it.

5th. He takes me to look at the Summer House.

8th. He cuts down two little trees & reads 'Chronicles' to me these evenings. Mr. Henry Marshall calls.

10th. A. reads 'Ezrah' & part of 'Nehemiah'. The children talk about the 'Son of God'. Lionel says, 'You know, Hallam, what it means. This is our Sun & God's Sun is much larger & brighter & is called Jesus Christ'. 'No', Hallam says, 'this is not it. We will ask Borton'.

A. reads me a little of Macnaghten on Inspiration. We talk until it is too late to finish 'Nehemiah'.

13th. A. chops wood for logs & we do finish 'Nehemiah'. Macnaghten. Maccabees.

15th. Sir John Simeon dines & sleeps & brings the children beautiful toys with which they are, of course, charmed. A. reads a bit of

'Arthur & Guinevere'. Sir John helps me to rig a boat for the children, walks with A. to the Needles & goes before our dinner. Maccabees in the evening.

17th. News of the taking of Canton Forts. We begin *Faust* as we have neither of us read it or anything German for a long time.

18th. News of Canton taken. We look anxious at debates about the Government of India. In the evening *Faust.*

21st. 'Defence of Guinevere'.

24th. Lord Dufferin sends his book to A. A. reads me 'Guinevere'. The head of the Derby Ministry comes.

25th. 'Deuteronomy', Hegel's *Philosophy of History,* Bede's *Ecclesiastical History* these evenings . . .

A kind letter from Mr. Helps with Outila [?]

March

1st. 'Guinevere'. A. pastes up part of the window to make me warm and makes a beautiful Snow Lady & puts a black hat on her. He reads to me about Arabia. He takes me to the Summer House and brings out the large bench & puts his cloak over me. Deliciously warm it is. I delight in the little rest. He reads me some of 'Guinevere' again because I ask again & again for it.

5th. He reads to me the Life of Caedmon in Bede. We agree as to its beauty & that this is the sort of biography we like. He says 'too late' to me.

I have not been at all well lately. Never was there such a tender nurse as my A. & the little boys follow his example & put cushions and make me comfortable after their fashion and are very pitiful over me & very loving to me. He makes the boys very happy by building castles that they may knock them down . . . A. blows bubbles in the nursery to keep the children from me & then he finds them so beautiful that he comes down to me with bubbles & children that I may see the gorgeous skies & the pretty little landships & the little planets breaking off from their suns & the single star becoming a double star. The boys wild with delight.

I find him lighting a fire for me. He reads part of *The Tempest* to me. A great delight. He paints the seats of the Summer House & reads me 'Guinevere'. Surely a most noble & touching poem. Sir

John dines. Very pleasant as he always is. Before he comes Lionel sits expecting him and says, 'I want John Simeon every day'. To-day he brings the boys two beautiful little boats with oars. Next morning he plays with the children & goes with A. to Totland to see the great blocks of Granite for the Lighthouse & leaves us before dinner. A. reads me a bit of Bacon's *Advancement of Learning*. Some passages as noble and beautiful as ever were written, I should think. Next day the Invalid chair comes from Sir John.

15th. Eclipse of the Sun. The day so cloudy that we see nothing of it except a darkness of evening for a few minutes. A. & the servants went on the down. There they saw the Sun red & the moon very near. A. has worked very hard at copying 'Guinevere' & brings it down to me finished at tea-time. The eve of our Lionel's birthday.

16th. The boys very happy with their ninepins. They are splendid, they say. A. plants yellow crocuses from pots to replace those eaten by mice that we may not miss our golden wreath this year. We have another in the South. He takes me out in the chair these days. Next day the Simeons kindly come to look after us. The first day she has left her baby so long.

A. reads me some Brown's *Atomic Theory,* 'Beneficence of Suffering' from the *Quarterly,* some of Lewes's *Goethe.*

22nd. Mr. Warburton comes for a night. One day the guns begin firing briskly from the forts while Lionel is on the down gathering flints. He throws them down & looking at the Moon overhead asks what the Man is going to do to them.

29th. Mr. Jowett comes. Next day he helps A. to draw me in the chair thro' Maiden Croft, St. George's Field, the Mead by the farmyard & the Park home.

31st. We have 'Sea Dreams' in the evening.

April

1st. Mr. Newman comes to tea and Mr. Jowett goes away with him afterwards to the Red House, so our delightful days with him as our guest end. Before he goes the children playing with him both fall in the grate. He snatches them up & they are not much hurt. A. reads the last chapters of 'Zechariah' to me. Mr. Jowett has been so very good to the boys & they so (I fear) excessively affectionate to him.

They will long remember their tossing in the blanket (M. Jowett's Shawl) which he and A. gave them in Mr. Jowett's room & their jumps in the carpet bags. The Druid Temples too. I have to make Druids for them.

A. takes me up to look at the summer house which he has painted & about our nine [*sic*] goes to Mr. Jowett.

5th. Storm of Rain & East wind. The weather-cock blown down. Next day Professor Tyndall & Harry Jones bring Mr. Pollock's book *New Friends* to Hallam. They & Mr. Jowett dine with us. Mr. Newman & Mr. Dicey come in the evening & are very agreeable. Rain & East wind continue.

8th. Professor Tyndall & Harry Jones call in the morning to take leave. Mr. Parker comes. Next day Mr. Jowett dines with us & Mr. Newman & Mr. Dicey come in the evening. We like them much.

A. paints the Summer house & Mr. Parker walks. He kindly promises to lend us books. Mr. Jowett, Mr. Newman & Mr. Wadly in the evening. Sir John Simeon.

13th. Mr. Parker leaves us. His high aspirations as a Publisher interest us very much. Mr. Jowett dines in the nursery & then goes up with A. to talk about the two poems he has read & to hear the third 'Guinevere'. A happy evening with A. He reads me about Dante in *Fraser* & some of the *Leaves of Grass* [by Walt Whitman] by way of curiosity.

14th. Bad news of my Father. I send him photographs of the boys. Two days later most joyful news of his wonderful recovery. Beautiful weather but still cold enough for me to be glad of the shelter of the hedges in the delicious spot where A. takes me where the bank is brilliant with primroses & celandine & the sweet briar begins to smell & the beautiful purple violets & where the birds sing.

A charming note from Mr. Jowett to the boys. We look at the newly planted trees in the belt & in these warmer days we go into Maiden's Croft, the garden & lawn. He reads a little Hegel to me. We hear of Mr. Moxon's illness. Some of Henry Taylor & some of the songs in *The Princess.* We hear nightingales these days & a cuckoo & I see a swallow. He reads to me some of the poems in Béranger's last volume & brings beautiful white nettle flowers which we agree would do well for capitals of pillars. It is a happy time for me with our little boys on each side of me on the sofa in the anti-room or Study reading to them nursery tales or nursery rhymes before our own evening reading. If it were not faithless I should be afraid of so much happiness as I have. A. reads me some of Kingsley's poems. I lie on the green bench near the Summer [house] while he plants the lilacs. He has drawn me in my little carriage all the way by himself except that I walked up our sandy road thro' the wilderness which this year he has covered all alone this year for the first time, I not having been well enough to help. Lady Simeon & Louy come just as we have returned home. We show them the beautiful flowers (Riviera Anemones, I think) growing wild in the plantation.

27th. After dinner next day A. & I talk of want of reverence for great men . . .

28th. The box of books which Mr. Parker so kindly promised to lend us arrives & among them Kemble's last book, a gift to A., also a garden net netted by my Father.

A. has the wood carved by William (Seaton) brought in for me to see. A. begins reading Motley* to me. A feeling of the freshness of youth comes over me. History read aloud recalls the feeling of the days when my Father used to read it aloud to me & my sisters.

After tea A. bids me go on with my music. He likes to hear me at it, he says. This too makes me think of all the pleasure my Father had in my music or rather in my singing as I did most evenings latterly to him but I cannot sing now. I sing to A. a little but am too weak and out of practice to sing decently. He takes me to look at the windows he has painted in the Summer [house]. I think they are beautiful.

May

1st. Books from Mr. Moxon. A beautiful present from Mr. Jowett. A Homer & a little Plato all bound in soft binding of Russian leather. We go on with Motley these evenings. It must be confessed that I think he is not just to Royal personages tho' on the whole his History is very interesting. We make a practice of looking [up] in Baxter all the flowers we do not know. It was pleasant to see the glee with which Hallam rushed up to Lionel the other day saying, 'Lionel, here is a crowfoot'. The boys answer the nice letter to them from

---

*John Lothrop Motley's (1814-77) *Rise of the Dutch Republic* (1856).

Mr. Newman & gather flowers to send him. Backgammon & I finish the English Hegel & read a passage in the German marked by Mr. Jowett.

7th. Hallam could scarcely be got to bed last night he is so delighted with Croker's stories from English History which I am reading to him. He is very sweet & simple & tractable. Backgammon, A. not equal to reading these two nights.

9th. A. takes me into the garden & Merwood shows us a lovely little nest of a white throat hanging suspended under the canopy of ivy which hangs from the wall near the back gates. A. reads to me about Oldcastle in Sharon Turner. Next day Mr. & Mrs. James White & Lotty & Clara & Mr. & Mrs. Blackwood lunch with us & the boys dine & are very good & have a famous romp with Lotty afterwards while the rest of the party go with A. to Alum Bay. A. talks to me when they are all gone as they do after evening tea. The day after he takes me to our Summer House in Maiden's Croft where I stay while he paints the floor.

13th. When we are out to-day he takes me from the summer house into the kitchen garden & the farmyard where Mrs. Merwood tells us some of the romance of the village. A. reads 'The Grandmother' to me.

15th. I have the large table desk put into his dressing room & he likes it there because it is lighter than his little study & he writes out 'The Grandmother' at luncheon. After dinner he fetches me to look at the view from the upper windows for the first time this year. Rich in its May beauty of golden gorse, flowering trees & yellow-green elms bathed in sunlight and green through the mist on the hills beyond the Solent a Cuyp-like* landscape.

Hallam begins his little History of England. He & Lionel dine with us at our luncheon & A. delights them by making them say bits of Greek. 'Say about a tree falling', 'Say Ye Mariners of England', 'Say about the Soldier sleeping & coming back to his dear home'.

19th. A. has to go to London to the dentist. The boys take me out, the Sardinian comes & the boys rush down for money as usual & Hallam brings his soldiers & Lionel his farm to show him.

I do A.'s books & make manuscript books for him & get many of the summer flowers put into the beds. Every day A. writes to me.

---

*In the style of the Dutch artist, Aelbert Cuyp (1605-91).

25th. He says he would most likely come but may take another day. I get flowers from him & let the children stay up beyond their usual time, but he arrives long after they are in bed. Next day we hang up the Chromes which he has brought with him in the Anti-room. Charles Weld comes & Mr. Fairbairn, & next day Mr. Henry Marshall dines with us & the next (June 1st) Mr. Wandby & the day after he comes in the evening & the day after Sir John Simeon & Col. Hall & then after this Mr. Wandby &, June 2nd, Charles Weld goes. Very kind & pleasant he has been. A. takes me to hear a nightingale. One has been singing in the withy bed but I fear its nest is stolen, it does not sing to-day. The May was like snow on the hedge and the rose campion made wreaths beneath them. The withies too wore white with their silky down. A most happy outing I have had. A. tells me his plan for the 'Maid of Astolat'.

June

2nd. He takes me to the Attic to see the Judas Tree & the Pink Thorn. The view wonderfully lifted up & fine, green lights on the slopes & many walls of rock seen not generally seen. We choose from Merwood's crooked oak sturdy wood for a chair which William Seaton is to make. We must put a seat under the Ilex near the front door for the Yarmouth view. Merwood tells us of a red-breasted nightingale which sings to them while working in the wood & comes hopping down among them. Also he tells us how he has been frightened by the flapping of the night hawk's wings when driving insects from the shelter of the trees. A. reads to me the recently published beginning of 'Hyperion' & we agree that it is the first. A snail on the drawing room window. We watch the blood flowing thro' it like smoke from head to tail. The children very much pleased. A. asks me at dinner whether I had ever put down Merwood's story of the Raven coming down on his white head when he was a Shepherd boy watching his flock. A. takes me out usual rounds & to our new seat under the Ilex. I never knew how glorious the woodbine could be until I saw it climbing high up the Ilex with the sunshine on it. But how beautiful everything looks & what delicious scents. I found a curious insect with saffron coloured worm-like body & a ruff of green wings round its neck. I opened the green closet in the study & Hallam exclaimed a worm! I found a melon-coloured oak caterpillar which had gnawed a hole more than an inch long & half an inch wide. The shavings were all round it.

9th. Poor A. has to go again to the dentist. Dreary work but his teeth must be attended to. I watch him off in the steamer. We have misty days. Lionel seeing a thick column of smoke go straight up says, 'how smoky God will be!' Hallam replied, 'Lionel, you should not talk so'. 'But it is true, Hallam, if all the smoke goes to Heaven, God will be as black as the funny man' (meaning the Ethiopian singer).

A. will have me drive every day & he writes every day. I send him some seringa & myrtle on our wedding day & Hallam insists on sending a bit of their cake.

One night I think I hear 'the villainous centre-bits'. I get up & listen & feel still more sure that there is a grinding of glass. I light a candle & show it at the window & grown bolder go to the window myself & see a snail whose shell is grinding the glass. Presently an almost musical note succeeds. Hallam finds a Jackdaw on the down which has apparently been wounded for it cannot fly. He is exceedingly anxious that Borton should know how to make raw meat when I tell him the bird eats it raw not roasted. The Simeons & Mrs. Prettyman kindly come to see me. She brings her son & her grandson & niece, also Mr. & Mrs. A. Court Holmes & Mrs. Bonvene & her sister & Miss Fanny Crozier all take pity on me. The boys make hay. Our violet-coloured Petunias & scarlet geraniums look very pretty with the Hay-cocks as a background.

23rd. I go early to the Ferry as A. says he may cross in an open boat. I wait about an hour & a half. Lady Hamond & Miss Caroline Hamond & Mrs. Grosvenor Hood come & talk to me. A. arrives in a little boat from the steamer. The country looks very pretty as we drive home. We find the boys still up waiting for him. The box of pictures sent by Mr. Palgrave opened in honour of his return.

A. takes me our happy rounds. We go first to the roses. Mr. James, Mr. Wood, & his cousin come. 'Jack' the Jackdaw flies away & is tempted back by a bit of meat when he is trying to get in at the nursery window. He stays a little while in his cage then flies away & we see him no more. We see the Bradleys again often now. Mr. Philpott and Mr. Martland also come. Mr. Holman Hunt arrives. He seems so good and great that one can dream oneself with an Artist of the olden-time. He races with the little Bradleys in the little cart & they & our boys have tea in the hay field. A pretty sight they are. Locker from Afton and Bouldnor call.

July

1st. Mr. Holman Hunt helps A. to trim the knee-feathers from the wreath of Elms over the sea view & to put a seat for me under the cedar. We go with the children to Captain Hamond's. They are wild with delight.

2nd. Mr. H. Hunt leaves us. Mr. Peel comes.

6th. Mr. Peel goes & Sir John Simeon, the Bradleys & Philpotts dine with [us].

Sir John leaves next day after luncheon & kindly wishes us to take Swainston on our way to Hampstead.

9th. We leave the well-loved place & arrive at Britannia Cottages. The Jesses have done their best for us but the situation is damp . . .

[The Tennysons take their children to London zoo; 'the Lions come & look at them make a low growl as if they thought them dainty morsels just out of reach'. Emily accompanies Alfred to Hull, where he takes a boat to Denmark in the midst of a great storm, much to her anxiety. However, he returns safely, and in London they visit the Crystal Palace, 'our Lionel struck almost dumb with wonder'.]

27th. We come home. A beautiful day. Admiral & Captain Crozier come on board the Steamer & I give the Admiral my red-lined cloak by way of flag & he waves it in honour of his little niece's birthday as we pass the house . . . All looks delightfully & smiling in the house. A. & I walk down to the Merwoods. A. reads me some of Lewes's *Goethe* & next evening Julian's rebuilding of the Temple.

September

1st. Mr. Rossetti, Captain Bridges, Mr. & Mrs. Dasent in these days. Mr. Wandby very ill. A. goes to see him. He gives his canaries to the boys to their great delight & leaves his fossils in A.'s care. We find Ladies' Tresses & Flowers which we like very much. Every possible day he takes me out in the little carriage & the boys are delighted if they are allowed to help. Certainly the pleasure of being drawn about our pretty fields by him is far greater than could [be] to me from most drives, fond as I am of driving. One morning I saw the little fellows in their blouses on the landing walking hand in hand playing at taking a morning walk & wild walk it was. I think I never saw them look prettier. I stood at the bottom of the flight of stairs & at every turn they rushed into my arms and Hallam calls me a great [asset]. Some pictures one longs to recall, one scarcely knows why. I am afraid it is a vain hope that if I live years hence these lines will recall this.

12th. A. goes up the Down to-night to see the Comet. I go with him to the Attic windows to look at it. It looked fine low down on the horizon over the beacon lights. Next day we call on the Bonvenes & the children go as far as the monument with A. on his way to Swainston. After dinner I play merry old dance tunes & the children dance. Lionel almost flying as usual. Hallam asked the other day whether the clouds were slippery; I ought to know for I was there before I came here. Next day he returns with Sir John & they come laden with Tomatoes which A. has begged for me because I had said that they suited me & ours are not yet ripe. They bring also the precious 'Sir Launcelot du Lac', so precious that I am afraid of having it in the house lest anything should befall it. They take me to Maiden's Croft in my little carriage & then Sir John reads me some of 'Sir Launcelot'. He has to return to guests at home. Next day A. takes me all along the foot of the Down to the road to Farringford Farm. The air is delightful. The only drawback lest it should be bad for him to drag me so far. In the evening both before & after tea he reads 'Sir Launcelot' to me.

'Sir Launcelot' again. The next day we have only been a little while in the Summer House, to which he has drawn me, when we hear Sir John's welcome tone & see him approaching with Mr. John Doyle. They all three join in dragging me up the down. A delightful day & to me a very enjoyable outing except that I feared to overwork them. We all four lie down & talk. The gentlemen go back with us & have a little smoke & chat with A. before they return. He reads me in the evening some of Winton's Preface about the *Sangraal.* Next day he reads about St. Sophia*. We are unsettled, expecting Mr. Palgrave. These days again at the foot of the down. We see a lizard & weasel running out of the hedge.

22nd. We have the pleasure so often longed for of welcoming Mr. & Mrs. Maurice. A. had just taken me round by Maiden's Croft & the ploughed fields & the lane & we were standing near the wood house when they arrived. A. reads 'Guinevere' after tea.

A rainy day so we send a note to Mr. Ludlow at the Warren Farm

---

*Hagia Sophia: St. Sophia at Constantinople, dedicated to the 'Logos' or Second Person of the Trinity; the Sacred Wisdom. The church was built 532-7.

instead of calling as we had intended. Sir John & Lady Simeon & Mr. John Doyle come to dinner. Very pleasant.

Next day Mr. Maurice comes down thinking to breakfast with the children & myself but we have already breakfasted. He is so good as to read Prayers for me. If one could but have them always read so! I never saw any except perhaps one who seemed so to commune with The Most High. Mr. Ludlow calls. Mr. Maurice & I drive with the children to the Lighthouse. The gentlemen walk. A sunny day. The gentlemen are so kind as to take the children down to the Needles. Mr. Maurice is so very kind to them. He loses his hat while taking care of them. We make unsuccessful attempts to clothe his head with handkerchiefs. Mr. Ludlow offers his hat and at last we see all three gentlemen walking wildly on the down without hats & then Mr. Ludlow takes them to the Farm & Mr. Maurice returns in his hat. He & A. take Hallam home by the down. Mr. Ludlow dines with us. Mr. Charles Anderson calls with Mr. Rossetti's card, walks with the gentlemen to Brook & comes in the evening. Mr. Maurice & I take the children to call on Mrs. Ludlow at the Warren Farm.

26th. Sunday, Mr. Maurice reads the morning service to Mrs. Maurice, A. & myself. Hallam is with us. A. rejoices as much as I do in his reading. A. reads some Milton to Mrs. Maurice & me while Mr. Maurice is at church—'Lycidas'.

Next day we prevail on them to stay a little longer. A. first takes me & then draws Mrs. Maurice in the little carriage to Maiden's Croft & when she has gone in they draw me up the down & home by the lane. Very pleasant talks in the evening. To-day Mrs. Maurice is too unwell to go in the little carriage. The gentlemen take me up the down again and the children with Borton go all the way to the Beacon with us. Mr. Maurice takes them by turns on his back! & they go with me by turns in the little carriage. Mr. Ludlow calls. Sir Alexander Grant, the Miss Ferriers & the Afton ladies come to tea. Harriet Wright arrives before dinner. A. reads 'The Grandmother' and 'Sea Dreams' in the dining-room after luncheon.

29th. Extremely sorry to part from Mr. & Mrs. Maurice. Who would not? Mr. Henry Marshall & Mr. Oliphant lunch with us and afterwards go in a boat to Alum with Sir Alexander & Miss Ferrier, who brings the children beautiful toys. Harriet goes, we do not, but A. takes me up by the down by the steps he has made for me, the children with us. He & I talk a long time after dinner.

30th. The comet splendid.

October

1st. These days Mr. Ludlow comes & Sir Alexander & Miss Ferrier & sometimes one or more of the Afton party. He reads 'The Grandmother'.

2nd. Sir Alexander & Miss Cotton want A. to walk with them but he in his goodness takes me up the down instead & afterwards he reads what he has done of 'The Maid of Astolat' and next day Sir Alexander & Miss Ferrier dine with us & he reads 'Guinevere', & Sir Alexander pronounces it the finest thing in the language. I know that it is said in the heat of a first hearing, still it is pleasant. We have the children taken out of bed to see the Comet. Lionel said to me next morning that he thought he was dead when he saw the comet & I was told that he said 'Am I dead?' These delightful outings on the down do me so much good & I think I feel better to-day than I have done these two years. To-day A. takes a volume of the *Morte d'Arthur* & reads me a noble passage about the battle with the Romans. Some *Mabinogion* in the evening. Next day we all call on Mrs. Austin at Plumbley's Hotel & see Mdlle. Von Zeschau. A. goes to meet Mr. & Mrs. Roebuck at dinner at Swainston. I decline. We see the Comet with Arcturus shining brightly over the nucleus, & when A. returns he comes to my room & tells me that it has been a glorious sight. He saw the Comet as he was driving to Swainston & then at dinner & he said he must leave the table to look at it & they all followed. They saw Arcturus give a great leap as he got out of the Comet's tail.

Col. Hall, Mr. Ludlow, Mr. Herbert, Captain & Mrs. Hamond call, Sir Alexander & the Miss Ferriers & Miss Cotton also. He helps A. to race me up & down the garden. Next day Mrs. Austin, Mdlle. Von Zeschau, Sir Alexander, Mr. Herbert & Mr. Ludlow dine with us. The Afton ladies in the evening. When the gentlemen have betaken themselves to the smoking room & Mrs. Austin has gone, we dance a set of Quadrilles! & sing & play. A. takes me a long way towards the Lighthouse next day, Mdlle. helping. Mr. Ludlow goes part of the way. A. reads us a little Milton, that part where Eve tempts Adam. Comet fainter but fine. We see it from the staircase window. A. from platform.

Next night A. draws Astronomical Diagrams for Harriet. The day after Sunday he reads the epistle & gospel & lessons & I the *Psalms*. It is too rainy & stormy for church. Again one of our delightful outings & we still see the Comet from the upper staircase window & from his Dressing-room window. A. is just going to read Shakespeare to us when Sir Alexander and his party arrive unexpectedly to tea.

12th. A. not very well but he takes me notwithstanding into the fields. Well that we had not gone further for the handle of the little carriage breaks. Edmund & Frank arrive. How delightful to have Frank back in England! We talk merrily. Next morning misty moisty. Edmund has brought us 'Frederic' to look at. Mrs. Austin & Mdlle. Von Zeschau lunch with us & Mrs. Austin talks to Frank about Malta among other things & is very agreeable. Sir Alexander & his party in the evening. A little music. Next day A., Edmund, & Frank take me to the milestone between the Beacon & the Lighthouse.

Up late talking in A.'s room & get up early this next day to see Edmund off. A. & Frank take me up the down. We wait for the children & see the white Afton pony in the lane & wait for the party there also. The children go with us to the Beacon. A. & Frank, Sir Alexander, the Miss Ferriers, & Mdlle. Von Zeschau go on, I very nearly to the Needles. A. stays with me, the rest of the party go on. A. sits beside me. Such a glorious afternoon. The sea calm & blue. Hurst Castle & the Red Lighthouses glittering each with a star on its forehead, the sands so yellow, the hills of every hue, nothing could be more exquisite. Frank soon comes up to us & he & A. race home with me. The splendour & glory of the sunset one cannot soon forget. The Crescent moon stood over our down as we turned into the Wilderness from Maiden's Croft. We asked all to dinner & Coggie rode off to Afton to invite the rest of the party there for the evening. A pleasant evening & late when the smoking party has left us. Frank sings to us. A. comes to send me to bed & then he reads 'The Grandmother' to the rest & to Frank what he has done of 'The Maid of Astolat'.

Next morning I get up early to breakfast with Frank who sets off for Brighton. Lionel standing by the window, Hallam hears him say 'dear Uncle Frank' for he has taken a great fancy to his Godfather. A. takes me out & we have a happy evening.

He reads 'The Rape of the Lock' to me.

17th. Next evening when Sir Alexander & Miss Ferrier come we show them that grand Sonnet of Michaelangelo's which we have been reading in Vasari, also the beautiful account of Raphael's power over the Artists. A. sends me to bed soon after ten & takes them up into the smoking room & reads 'The Maid of Astolat'.

18th. Mrs. Austin, Sir Alexander Grant & the Miss Ferriers come to say goodbye. Next day being rainy A. has a romp with the boys & reads bits of 'Sir Launcelot' to me. Some of *Julius Caesar* after dinner & scraps of *Noctes Ambrosianae* after tea. I take Harriet to the Ferry next day & afterwards A. reads some Milton to Matilde (Mdlle. Von Zeschau) and me. He reads the *Psalms* with Hallam & me on Sunday morning & we go to church in the afternoon. *The Merchant of Venice.*

28th. A letter about Mr. W. Moxon's extraordinary statements. Two decisive letters answering soon found by me but the affair occupies nearly all our time & thoughts for some days. So much writing has to be done. Hallam with Bowerbird notions of adornment not being able to get flowers because of the rain scatters scraps of all kinds about the hall & the stairs in honour of Nanny's birthday & Lewis Fytche's wedding day. Next day Sir John Simeon dines & sleeps here & is as usual most sympathetic. A. reads the *Psalms* with us & lessons & epistle & gospel to us. He takes me out as usual every fine day. To-day the sun shines brightly & the birds sing sweetly.

Two very welcome gifts of late, Gladstone's *Homer* from Sir Alexander Grant and Müller & Donaldson's *Greeks* from Mr. Parker.

November

1st. From eleven to eleven we are looking for Moxon letters instead of being at Westfield where we are asked for the opening of the Ryde Museum. Charles Weld & Mr. Forster most kind in taking all sorts of trouble for us in this Moxon business. Nevertheless we have another weary day of letter hunting & letter writing. The great Ilex opposite the dining room planted in the year of the battle of Waterloo has split. This split is filled with clay & it is girded by strong iron chains & soon moves itself by its branches.

We are very happy every evening almost in the Study, the boys & myself on our three chairs side by side an arm round each & I reading 'Reynard The Fox' to them. A. reads *A Midsummer Night's Dream* & some of Sir Francis Palgrave's.

6th. Matilde & Miss Gordon come to Maiden's Croft & tell us of the birth of Lady Gordon's daughter.

9th. We go to look at Merwood's new purchase of Sheepwash Farm.

A pretty spot. I glad to find that Oreb's spring runs thro' the green of which A. is Lord. So he who is so fond of a running stream is not quite without one. In the evening he reads me all that is done of 'The Maid of Astolat'. I get cloth & lining & have a cloak made to replace that which he has lost by way of surprise, but he has seen the bill for the cloth & noticed my sending out a bundle of dark wash!

10th. My Father's birthday. The children & I write to him & send white roses.

Next day I am busy preparing for his departure. A bitter east wind so he thinks that I must not go even to the Ferry, & of a journey to London for me he will not hear, & so he goes alone I finish Palgrave, go on with Thorndale, then read Ludlow's lectures on India with great interest, & also *Richard II*, & among other things I play Welsh airs to the boys & sing 'Too Late' to them. It is wonderful to see their faces of awe and sadness listening, Hallam by my side, Lionel on the oak chair near the Piano.

Play at 'Earth, Air & Water', a great favourite with them especially as it ends in a great romp & laughter. They bring me word that a very large Eagle looking almost a man on the down has been seen. Every day letters from A. reporting progress of Moxon business which is we hope satisfactorily settled. Miss Gordon & Mdlle. Zeschau, of whom I have seen a good deal & like much, come to say farewell (19th).

20th. A. arrives to-day and brings Mrs. Gatty with him, reads 'The Grandmother' to her, goes to the shore with her to look for sea Anemones of which she leaves some with a Chiton when she herself leaves on the 24th. A. has read 'Maud', 'Nimuë' & 'Locksley Hall' to her. He reads some of Ludlows' *India* to me.

27th. We get news of the settlement of the Moxon affair, thanks to Charles Weld's energetic kindness. A.'s cold so bad we have to betake ourselves to our own books in the evening. He is reading Huc's *China** & tells me about it. Mrs. Gatty has already kindly sent us her 'Poor Incumbent' which touched us both. She now sends her *Legendary Tales* & Mr. Gatty a volume of Sermons. The Chiton has taken to walking about the finger glass, we find, but no one sees that mysterious beastie in the act.

---

*Evariste Régis Huc (1813-1860); a Lazarist; after ordination he went to China in 1839 as missionary and wrote *Le Christianisme en Chine*, etc., 4 vols., 1857-58.

December

1st. A. & I sufficiently recovered from our coughs to get out again. He mows, for a scythe arrives from Mrs. Gatty bright as a sword.

7th. A. reads me interesting things from the *Times* & tells me to read the Queen's 'Proclamation to India'. Deeply interesting of course to us both. Hallam reads to him & A. reads me what he has written of 'The Maid of Astolat' & Huc & begins *Frederic the Great* to me. Mrs. Cameron's gift & a great deal of letter writing lately. I play a little at battledore & shuttlecock with A.

20th. Mr. Palgrave after A. has taken me into Maiden's Croft & brings a most welcome gift from Sir Francis & himself, Milman's *Latin Christianity,* a book I had just been saying we ought to have, and all kinds of presents for the children. Our mask of Dante comes which Mrs. Prinsep has kindly had mounted for us & we put it up in the lobby. A. reads some *Frederic.*

24th. Mr. Woolner comes. The boys wild with excitement at seeing him.

25th. The Gentlemen blow bubbles for the boys the day being rainy. Mr. Masson sends his *Life of Milton & Essays.* Mr. Conington, A. reads some *Samson Agonistes.* The boys rejoice in the glorious sunrise after the rainy days. The boys & I see Mr. Palgrave off. A. & Mr. Woolner take me out after Mr. Woolner has in the morning worked hard at my Medallion as he did yesterday and for all these days. We have now made the Dining-room his studio where he finds the light better. A. reads a little of *Comus.* He tells the boys stories at luncheon.

1859

January

1st. Letters from the dear ones at Grasby. Mr. Woolner still hard at work. A. reads some Milton to us.

4th. A., Emily, & Mr. Woolner take me to the beacon. A. covers me with his great cloak & leaves me only a peephole but I enjoy my outing very much on this bright party day. He reads part of 'Enid' to us. Next day Mr. Woolner finishes the medallion & A. finishes reading 'Enid' to us & I rejoice that it seems to me so beautiful.

The day after this Mr. Jowett arrives & the boys hail him as if they had only parted from him yesterday. The day after this Mr. Woolner goes. The freshness & imaginativeness of his talk have struck me this time more than ever.

18th. Julia Cameron's wedding day. Mr. Jowett goes. We have had very interesting conversations with him, & A. & he have had long walks & A. has read on different evenings 'The Grandmother', 'The Maid of Astolat', part of the *Two Noble Kinsmen,* a scene from Thiery where he sees Ordetta going to the Temple, some of Shakespeare's sonnets, Gray's 'Elegy', Crabbe's 'Parting Hour', the Song of the Maid of Astolat & some of Goethe's Poems. One evening Hallam was promoted to the honour of reading 'The Lad who went to the North Wind' & one evening Sir John Simeon & his brother Cornwall dined with us, & tho' I have not been able to go on the down with them, A. tells me of the magic lights. Mr. Parker sends us *Man & His Dwelling Place* & A. reads me a little of it two evenings & he & Hallam take me to see the first snowdrops.

20th. We read from cantos of the *Pugatorio* together.

Next day we have worse news of Mr. Hallam. He is taken from us the day after & the world is the poorer. Rainy & stormy. Hallam reads all but the Absolution of the service. One Sunday before he volunteered to read the Litany and he took the clergyman's part, Lionel the clerk's most devoutly.

Next day A. takes me to see a fallen tree. The hole it has left is nearly filled with water. Two then fallen in the belt & one broken. A. picks up a poor little dove which is walking feebly along. I take it on my knee but it dies in the afternoon which makes us as well as the boys sad.

25th. We hear particulars of Mr. Hallam's death. Hallam asks if he may wear mourning for him. He helps A. now with my little carriage. Both boys seem much interested in Kingsley's *Heroes of Greece* which I am reading to them.

February

1st. A letter from Mrs. Cator telling of her Father's legacy. Every evening we read the *Purgatorio* & one night a bit of the 'Maid of Astolat' to me.

8th. He has quite finished writing it down now all but a little bit at the end & brings it to me for I want to read it to myself. It is well to read things to oneself without the glamour of his reading which may beguile one.

Next day 'Old England' & Liddell's *Dictionary* come from Mr. Jowett. The boys charmed with 'Old England'. A. reads to me some of *In Memoriam* & talks about it. Very delightful. The day after Mr. Gatty comes. He interests us by telling us of Dr. Hook & of his own curate who has made forty youths deemed untameable obedient to him in all things . . . A. reads 'Locksley Hall' & 'The Grandmother' to him & when he leaves on the 12th he takes 'The Grandmother' with him to be printed with 'The May Queen' for the people.

14th. Happy evening among happy evenings. He reads me 'Boädicea' & part of 'Maid of Astolat'.

21st. We finish the *Purgatorio* & A. to-night & other nights after this reads me some Burns & he & the boys bring me violets, primroses, daffodils, lovely nosegays day by day. I begin *Robinson Crusoe* to the children. Hallam highly delighted. Next day we mark the places for the trees & shrubs which we have got from Williams & the days following look to the planting & send for more . . .

23rd. Sir John Simeon, Captain Bonvene, & Mr. Eyre Powell dine with us. A. reads me the VIII Chapter of *Romans* in Greek with Mr. Jowett's commentary. Another evening some of the *Times* Leaders & I read Sir J. Pakington's speech on the Navy Estimates with great interest. The boys most careful over me because of my cough. Hallam keeping me from draughts and from talking & reading, & prescribing medicine & plaster, dear little Lionel applying his remedy of pats on the back, in which he cannot help rejoicing a little. A. brings me a hyacinth in a pot & a beautiful nosegay. He reads me the 2nd Chapter of *Colossians* with the Greek. Other nights we have had Backgammon. He has walked by starlight on the Down.

Tina Garden & Matilde arrive & walk with Mr. Eyre Powell & his friend VanderKisten who want A. to dine with them on St. Patrick's day but he declines. We put up the Roman Photographs of the Sybils & Modesty & Vanity given us by Mr. Arthur Butler, also the *Edinburgh* & Louy Lushington & Henry Hallam's portraits.

March

16th. Our Lionel's birthday. He is pleased with his flowers. Matilde gives him a little music & A. & I have a little Blindman's buff with the boys. Hallam looks on Lionel with a kind of awe to-day & asks me if I order dinner on his birthday, knowing that I order Sunday's dinner on Saturday & thinks this day sacred too & so it is to us. A. reads some of Shakespeare's Sonnets. Next day Mr. Garden arrives.

19th. The Gardens go. Next day A. too languid to read. We look at the Physical Atlas. A. reads 'Guinevere' to us & the next day, the 22nd, Hallam & I take him to the Ferry for London to look after the publication of the four *Idylls*. A magic music with the boys.

Matilde most kind in taking care of me. In the evenings she reads me some of the *Morte d'Arthur* & one of Robertson's Sermons on Sunday & the Falcon.

April

2nd. Matilde goes on the 2nd & I am sorry to lose her. Daily letters from A. He cannot return before Monday because Mr. Watts is too ill to finish his second portrait which every one pronounces better than the first good as that is considered. He returns looking well & cheerful & he brings Nimuë with him. He has seen a great many people in Town. He dines with Mr. Chapman at his club, is introduced to Mr. Tom Hughes who delights him, sees Mr. Ruskin for the first time. He reads his 'Guinevere' to the Duke & Duchess of Argyll at Argyll Lodge. Reads *Idylls* at Little Holland House and to many others. He reads one or both *Idylls* to the Somerses & all at Little H. House, to Mr. Venables, Mr. Hughes, Mr. Woolner, Mr. Patmore, Charles Weld, Mrs. Norton & Mr. Norton (her son). He sees Mr. Palgrave, Mr. Barrett, the Proctors, Lady Ripon. He dines with Mr. Owen, meets Dr. Farre. He is touched by Lord Lansdowne's, at his age, coming to call on him. He is introduced to the Duc d'Aumale who comes to Little H[olland] H[ouse] to have his portrait taken. He likes HRH & means to send him some of the Tobacco which Aunt Franklin brought for himself from the East. Mr. Woolner brings Mr. Novello to see him. Very pleasant that he should get to know these great practical men, Mr. Edward Villiers and the Burns-Joneses one day at Little Holland House.

8th. Rather a wild night & day of pain but it is almost worth while to have the pain to be so tenderly nursed as I am by A. 'Nimuë', some of *Don Juan* these two evenings. Mr. Warburton dines & stays the night.

Mr. Dodgson comes in the morning & to tea in the evening. Mr. Lear's six songs come, 'The time draws near', 'Come not when I am dead' seem to us the best & wonderfully beautiful. Sir John Simeon & Mr. Dodgson dine with us & Mr. Dodgson shows his photographs. A. & I read a little of the *Gododin* another evening some of *The Tempest* & the Balcony scene in *Romeo & Juliet*. The Welds & Mr. Barrett come. One night when Mr. Barrett has left A. reads the Flight in Carlyle's *French Revolution*. Mr. & Mrs. Butler & Mr. Galton here. Arnold calls to see about the Oriel windows in the Attics suggested by Charles Weld & the vaulting of the ceilings.

May

1st. The Welds go. Very pleasant has their visit been. Charles takes 'Guinevere' up with him & also 'Riflemen'. I have a happy evening with my A. correcting the proofs of 'The Maid of Astolat'. Mr. Archibald Peel comes.

8th. Proofs of 'Guinevere' come.

10th. Arnold & his men begin the alterations in the Attics. We all go up, A. & I & the boys to see the work of destruction begin. Poor little room it is sad for A. & me when we see its barn-like rafters & we grow quite sentimental over it when A. talks of all the pleasant evenings spent under its low ceiling, all the thoughts & all the feelings thought & felt there.

12th. Sir John Simeon and Sir George and Lady Baker dine with us. Sir John bring the *Times* with a leader about it and Lady Baker sings . . . Sir John sings old English airs to Mr. Peel & A. upstairs. We have heard that Sir Alexander Grant's brother is killed in action in India.

14th. Mr. Peel takes a stanza of 'Up, Jack Tar' for Balfe to set.

15th. A great putting out of Greenhouse flowers. I fix the places, Hallam carries out some plants, & A. digs the holes. The following days we are busy with the Attics & A. takes Hallam & me up to the platform as best he can in its unfinished state.

23rd. We hear of his bust having gone to Trinity, Cambridge. The next day the last pane of the new window in his study is put in & he calls me to hear a nightingale from it when open. A delightful inauguration. The Duke & Duchess of Argyll walk with A. & dine with us. A. reads his Poems of '52. A very pleasant evening. Next day they all three go geologizing to Brook. I not strong enough yet. The Duke & Duchess dine with us. A. reads 'Maud' afterwards. We must part from them to-night as they go early tomorrow. One does not like to think of their working so hard.

For some days we take his proofs to the Summer House to correct. Sir John comes and he likes our alterations in A.'s study very much. A. wishes me to play my settings of 'Hands all Round' & 'Riflemen Form!' to him. I am glad that he likes them & much more than glad that he himself does. He reads me the 1st Act of *Macbeth* & next night some of the *Morte d'Arthur* where Launcelot behaves so courteously & Sir Palomides so uncourteously & where Arthur goes to see La Beale Isoude.

29th. Mrs. Norton & Mr. & Mrs. Brinsley Norton come in the evening after having called in the morning. Mrs. Norton very gentle & kind.

31st. I am called up by A. to see the view from the attic window before the sash is put in. It is really enchanting. We are told that the wretched farmers poison the birds here. If the dear things must be killed let it be mercifully & so that they may serve for food.

June

2nd. Mr. & Mrs. Theodore Martin call and dine with us next day. After dinner we discover that she is the famous Helen Faucit. She interests me much. Both are very agreeable. Another day Giotto's Chapel at Padua & Perugino's St. Sebastian chromographs come to us from Mr. Prinsep. All these days we take the proofs up to the Summer House.

6th. Merwood tells us of bees in the roof of the stable. Mr. Lear comes to us in the Summer House. A great pleasure to see him looking so well and cheerful. A. & he walk & he sings in the evenings & A. reads to him 'The Maid of Astolat' with which he is delighted as he is with 'Guinevere' which he reads to himself. Mr. Evans arrives. Mr. Lear sings. A. read 'The Grandmother' & next day they walk & Mr. Lear sings to us & we square words. A. tells me not to look at the window until its crown is on.

10th. He has to go to London about the Proofs & to the Dentist. I ask Captain & Mrs. Bonvene to dinner because Mr. Lear knows so many of his friends & relations & the Miss Oldershaws in the evening. Mr. Lear sings & the Captain & he talk much together. Next day I get up early to breakfast with Mr. Lear. When he goes

Lionel looking out of the window says, ‘How I like him’, & one echoes the words in ones heart. Alfred Crowquill calls but does not come in.

13th. Hallam draws rose trees & myrtle & orange trees for A. & I send him myrtle & seringa flower. Letters as usual from A. I am very venturesome. I have opened a door into the greenhouse during his absence.

Mr. Rawnsley & Drummond arrive unexpectedly. They go next day in a boat to the Needles & are charmed especially with the arched rock at Scratchell's Bay. They go after luncheon. Most kind they have been. My A. writes to me that both sights & sounds were magnificent at the Handel Festival to which he has been. It has been one of the desires of my life to hear *The Messiah* grandly performed. Delight that it should have been fulfilled in him. One day he went to the British Museum with Frank. Another he was at Stafford House.

The tailor puts up the bed, all the workmen & many besides work with might & main but the house is not made beautiful as I had wished for A.

27th. He comes. Never I think so happy a meeting for me of all the happy meetings. He likes all that is done. I have warned him beforehand how much was undone. I let the boys show him the new door from the study to the Greenhouse according to my promise to them, and he is pleased with everything. The view from the new windows is a kind of drunkenness of delight. Mrs. Cameron has come with him & also likes the alterations.

28th. Sir Pelleas and Ettarre to us after our pleasant talk. Next day Frederic arrives. He & A. walk on the down. A. kicks against a hedgehog & brings it in. We feed it with bread and milk which it takes & rolls itself up.

July

1st. Mrs. Cameron goes. Frederic crosses with her. Meanwhile Hallam & I call on Captain & Mrs. Hamond in their new house. Very charming it is. A. will delight in the lawn. Their little Carry says ‘Break, Break’ to me in such a touching sweet voice. While the Grants & Mr. Ferrier are dining with us there is a fearful thunder storm, hailstones as big as Walnuts, the kitchen two or three inches deep in water which comes into nearly every bedroom. Merwood pierces holes in the bathroom ceiling to let the water off & so preserve the ceiling. Just before the storm begins Mrs. Cameron's Ellen arrives to our astonishment. She is sent to ask for the manuscript of 'Guinevere'. A. does not care about his manuscripts. He gives them to anyone who asks. To me they are more precious than words can say. Every page almost a memory. He is so good as to say that if I do not like to part from it and he has promised it, he will copy it out rather than that I should have to part from it. Mrs. Cameron thought the Grants were to have 'Guinevere'. A. says she shall have it if anyone has it. One does not like to refuse kind & energetic Mrs. Cameron anything.

3rd. Sir Alexander & Lady Grant leave [. . .]. There are few we should so unwillingly lose. Sir John comes.

Next day Frederic leaves us for Jersey & the next the poor James Whites who have lost their daughter come to stay with us. Dear & good people, how bravely they bear up under their great loss.

10th. The *Idylls* come. Splendid weather this week since the storm.

11th. The Whites leave us. Next day Sir John dines with us. The Bradleys & Mr. Duckworth come in the evening & he sings to us.

14th. The Fields from Boston, USA, come to us. She with a face like the old Italian Masters' faces. Very attractive. Next day the Bradleys also dine with us. We have news of the Peace which we fear bodes no good for England.

27th. We go to Park House & then to the Camerons at Ashburton Cottage.

August

3rd. We see Frederic, the Prescotts, & Mr. Stephen Spring-Rice and his daughter Mary.

On the 16th we part from A. at the Waterloo Station . . .

[Alfred travels with Palgrave and F. C. Grove to Lisbon. On his return to London, meets Alexander Macmillan the publisher, 'with whom he is much pleased'.]

October

27th. Mr. Charles Sumner from America dines with us and is very agreeable. When he leaves next day Lionel, as if he had foreboded his fate, said, 'If a naughty comes and hurts Mr. Sumner, I will fight him and die myself for him'.

31st. A. sends 'Sea Dreams' to Macmillan for his Magazine. Next day Frank is prevented from crossing by the storm & goes again next day. A drearily short visit. Mr. & Mrs. Lewis & Mr. & Mrs. Gatty. He has been lecturing at Barnesley & Chichester on A.'s poems & has found warm response especially at Barnesley. 'Sea Dreams', 'Guinevere', some of Shakespeare's sonnets, 'The Vision of Sin', & talk.

November

5th. Mr. & Mrs. Gatty go. We have had many trees blown down. Notwithstanding the storm. A. & boys go out to see the splendid bonfire which by A.'s care has been kept smouldering for days, Frank helping while here.

8th. Mr. & Mrs. Kingsley come. Miss Heathcote came yesterday. The boys very happy with Mr. Kingsley. He and A. burn the Guy Fawkes when Henry has made one for the boys. Miss Heathcote goes, very kind & amusing she has been. The Kingsleys leave us on the 10th. Very much have we liked having them. They have been delighted with Alum Bay & have I hope enjoyed the down up which she went on the donkey. Mr. Parker arrived yesterday & A. read 'Maud'. A. goes to Alum Bay with him to-day after having picked up sticks with the boys. Next day Mr. Parker goes to Mr. Helps. We go to look at the grave of Hallam's poor little canary found dead in its cage on my Father's birthday. Its poor little companion made mournful cries. We see two swallows while in the garden to-day. A. reads *Richard II* magnificently to me. Another day *Henry IV*.

19th. Hallam & I go with A. to the Ferry on his way to see Mr. Cameron off for Ceylon. He brings back Mrs. Cameron & Charlie & Henry & Ellen with him next day.

Sir John Simeon dines with us one evening, he and Mr. Charles Wynne another. A. reads 'Guinevere' to them. Mr. Kingsley sends Hallam 'The Good-natured Bear'. Mr. Estcourt comes to see what can be done about purchasing these houses which may spoil our view of the sea. Mrs. Cameron has an agreement with Ling giving her the option of purchasing Linglands. She and Charlie & Henry go to-day (30th), most kind as usual she has been. A. much interested by Darwin's book which Mr. Palgrave is so good as to send him, not knowing we have already a copy.

December

The Illustrated Princess comes. Beautifully got up but the Illustrations we cannot admire. A. has mounds raised & trees planted to hide Knight's house & we look after them. In the evenings when we are alone he reads me some of the 'Arthur & Merlin' lent us by Sir John. On the 14th he brings me down his 'Tithonus'. Snow two feet thick, but the sun warm, perfect winter day. He takes me out & sweeps a path for me and we have 'Tithonus' in the evenings. Our globes arrive. Sir John dines with us & brings the boys White's *Natural History,* recommended by Owen as the best first-book, as a gift. They delighted.

Mr. Ellis sends a sumptuous present of choice wines which everyone admires even Mr. Novello when he comes some days later. A. reads me part of the journal in the Cornhill written by one of the officers of the *Fox*. Mr. Palgrave arrives & he and A. play with the boys after dinner on Christmas day & the Christmas Tree which Elizabeth has kindly prepared as a surprise looks rather magical in the Antiroom when we open the drawing room doors. One evening they have Magic Lantern. Charles Weld, Mr. Woolner, Mr. Jowett arrive. Sir John & Mr. Charles Wynne come to luncheon & bring an engraving from the English Cenci supposed to be the original Guido, Mr. Wynne's gift to A.

1860

January

2nd. Mr. & Mrs. Bradley dine with us. A cheerful evening. Next day Mr. Palgrave goes & one feels that a friend has gone. Mr. Woolner delights the boys with his stories for which he has wonderful faculty of invention.

One evening reads 'Revelation' thro' to us. Very glad we are that A. has been able to persuade Mr. Jowett to stay longer on condition that he may breakfast early alone so as to get to work in good time. They walk together. In the evening Maken, the young soldier who had stopt them to ask where A. lived, came by appointment. Very intelligent he seemed. A. gave him a copy of *The Poems & The Princess* & wrote their names in them. Mr. Jowett translates some of *The Apology*. Very delightful to us both & for two more evenings we have it. The evening after A. reads some old Ballads to us after we have all been to Jane's room to listen to some mysterious sounds in the wall. Next evening A. reads the Balcony scene in *Romeo & Juliet*. The boys dine at our luncheon time. Mr. Jowett tells them the story of Ulysses. They listen entranced. Mr. & Mrs. A. Court Holmes call just as Mr. Jowett is going. Sorry indeed we are to say good bye to him. A. reads me some Keats.

Next day he walks with Mr. Bradley & says that he has never been out on a more delightful day on the down. The sunset gorgeous & the stars at night splendid. The Bonvenes go. A pity that one cannot keep pleasant neighbours. A. reads me some MacKintosh.

February

1st. Mrs. Cameron arrives with two legs of Welsh mutton from Eastnor. We say that it is against our rule to receive gifts from her, dear, generous creature that she is, but she persists. Sir John Simeon & Sir James & Lady Carmichael call A. reads me some of Victor Hugo's '[Les] Petites Epopées' lent us by Sir John.

The Bradleys call to take leave. Sorry are we. Another delightful evening reading. A. reads 'Amos' to me.

The poor little Squirrel given to the boys by Afton escapes while Henry is cleaning the cage. He throws a stick up at it to bring it down from a tree which kills [it] and makes us all sad. It had such pretty ways. We were all fond of it.

13th. Heard arrives & we engage him. Glad to have a first-rate gardener. A. & I look to pulling down part of the sheep pen & cutting down trees. We make a door from our bedroom to the bathroom. A. goes on with the 'Epopées' to me these evenings. I read *Pilgrim's Progress* to the boys which delights them.

March

1st. Mrs. Cameron brings a vivid blue paper with a border from the Elgin Marbles. The vivid blue neither she nor we like. We as usual protest against her prodigal kindness.

6th. The foundations of the Lodge in the Orchard begun to be dug. Boswell's *Johnson,* Froissart, Clarke's *Homer,* Smith's *Dictionary* arrive from Mr. Jowett. The Froissart he most kindly gives. The loan of the rest right welcome. 'Epopées', 'Adam Adair' and other small poems.

14th. We choose the [sheets] for the Lodge & after the next day I do not leave my room for more than a month.

16th. On our Lionel's birthday the boys bring me the flags we have given them by us & all their other gifts. The Camerons spent the day with him, and tho' Lionel has longed for the day for months he said that it had not disappointed him.

Unknown to me A. sends for the Newport doctor. In time we are told that we have whooping cough. The boys take it about a fortnight after me & Elizabeth about a fortnight after them. We are shut up in three separate rooms. Fortunately the boys' opens into mine. Their nurse & I have had the cough before & I have never been beyond our own grounds. It is supposed to have come from the beautiful paper with which I papered our room knowing that he would like it. On trial it was found to contain a great quantity of Arsenic and so it was soon as might be stript off the wall. A. puts off all the guests he can from staying in the house but I am glad that Mr. W. Clark from Cambridge, Mr. Woolner, Mr. Crowe, and Mr. Venables do venture to come and that the Duke and Duchess of Argyll who stay at the Hotel spend three evenings with him. Lord Lorne one & Mrs. Cameron & Mrs. Bailey many.

A. often brings me flowers and one day digs up a large root of primroses and plants them in the big Terra Cotta vase which was tumbled on my arm from its stand before my marriage & has made [it] I fear less useful for life. Now I have the happy primrose memory instead of the unhappy accident one. Mrs. Cameron & Mrs. Bailey are so kind as to bring the boys all sorts of things to amuse them & all our friends around are most kind & two of those who have to work in the day sit up with the boys at night.

April

16th. A. brings me down into the drawing room & then Hallam unexpectedly to me & with Mr. Wallworth leaves. Our Lionel comes, so here we all are once more, thank God. How beautiful everything looks. There is enchantment about all. I dine with A. & have tea & the boys come down after dinner. Tomorrow A. has to go to his dentist.

25th. He returns & brings Hine with him about furniture for Brights' House (The Terrace).

27th. He reads me 'Boädicea'. He digs a good deal in the garden & we look after what Heard is doing in the Terrace grounds & the making of the Terrace & about the furnishing & fitting of it. Mrs. Cameron coming from Town rushes in with a catalogue which she thinks will be helpful even before she has seen her children.

30th. Mr. Scoones our Twickenham clergyman comes.

May

2nd. Mr. Fellowes calls & afterwards Lord Dufferin who interests us extremely by telling us of Cyril Graham's discoveries of the 87? White marble cities in the black basaltic land of the Koran with their inscriptions in an unknown tongue.

A. reads to me very interesting things from the *Quarterly*. The poor boys wild with delight at getting out again. Mrs. Cameron takes A. into her house where he finds the officers of the Fort drawn up to be introduced. He offers the Major our stables & begs that he will put a married sergeant whom he does not well know what to do with in the rooms over.

Mr. Chapman & Mr. Garden come to stay & Mrs. Cameron in the evening. A pleasant heart-warming evening. They go next day.

13th. Mrs. Cameron wants to give us one of her lucky purchases of pictures, but we will not take it. These days he takes me out & mows. Next day Mr. Dempster arrives & sings. He goes next day. The draft of the Terrace road which Mr. Chapman has kindly drawn comes to-day & his gift of Thackeray's Christmas stories. A. reads some Froissart to me. Eugene [Hay Cameron] arrives from Ceylon. A. mows.

19th. A very pleasant surprise this morning. A most kind letter to A. from the Prince Consort with a request that he will write his name in HRH's copy of the *Idylls*.

20th. Eugene suddenly summoned and goes. Henry Taylor comes. A. goes to see him at the Camerons. He comes up to Farringford with Mrs. Cameron but may not come in until he has Queen's leave. A. takes me into Maiden's Croft & they go with us. The delight of our beautiful home is as great to-day as on the day he first brought me to it.

25th. The photographs of Mr. Woolner's Llandaff statues come & the casts of Michael Angelo's last work & the Phidian Victory fastening her Sandal. I rejoice to think that the children will become early familiar with these wonderful works. Mr. Woolner's must, I should think, be a great statue and also his St. Paul tho' he is not quite my St. Paul.

28th. Dr. Thompson comes. Very glad to see A.'s old friend & delighted to have the James G. Marshalls next day. We gather a new white flower in the wilderness which neither we nor our guests know & the boys very excited at the idea of seeing Godmama & spend the day in gathering flowers & arranging them. Cast of the Venus of Milo comes. Charles Weld arrives.

June

2nd. We made arrangements with Keeping to go geologizing with the gentlemen to Brook next day. Mrs. Marshall & I meet them on Afton Down. They go on the 3rd. I fear that their visit has not been so enjoyable as we would fain have made. There are none to whom we would more willingly give pleasure. The white & red thorn & Laburnums in full beauty. A. flies Hallam's kite with him from the top of the house. A. reads some 'Elaine' to me & next day flies kites with the boys on the Down.

7th. Dr. Wolff comes. A wonderful inspiration in some of his stories. He looks mild & kind and is very courteous to us & very thoughtful for us.

10th. He preaches in the church in the morning & reads prayers to us in the afternoon & expounds a part of the 51st Psalm. Very interesting. The boys most attentive. He addresses himself a good deal to them. Some of the servants also present.

13th. Hallam says you must go out with us to Maiden's Croft and see our kites fly for you are a bride & Papa a bridegroom. Mr. & Mrs. Isaacson, Mr. Filton, & Mrs. Cameron dine with us and all except myself go to hear Dr. Wolff's lecture in the schoolroom which Mr. Isaacson has kindly lent us. A. walks with Mrs. Cameron & so is later than the rest of the party who drive. Mr. Isaacson tells the assembly that he only waits for A. & they cheer. Six pounds are collected for Dr. Wolff's church & the boys, when they hear of the church building, rush off to their purses & give all they have except Grandpapa's sovereign. Poor Lionel has lost his & Hallam gives his money every week till it is restored to him.

14th. Dr. Wolff goes. A. accompanies him to Yarmouth, hears that the Emperor of the French wants eleven millions with which to fortify France, and that the Isle of Wight is to be fortified. Frank & Mr. Lear come. Mrs. Cameron, Mr. Arthur Prinsep, Miss Kate Perry in the evening. I hear a tramping on the drive when I am resting after dinner and think it is Americans coming as seven did the other day to ask for admittance but find that it is Mrs. Cameron's Grand piano which she has most kindly sent for Mr. Lear. It is pleasant to see the surprise of each one coming in & seeing it. The Camerons in the evening. Mr. Lear sings a long time.

Next day I get up early to see him & Frank off for they must go to-day. Mrs. Cameron, Arthur Prinsep, Perry dines with us and we have from him the extremely interesting story of his escape, all alone in the Indian Mutiny when only seventeen.

We are busy looking to the furnishing of the Terrace which we have bought to save the view of the sea as much as possible & to the building of the Lodge in the orchard. Arthur Tennyson with his bride, Arthur Wright & his Mary Ker & Aunt Mary Anne all visit us & at the Camerons, Lady Somers & Henry Taylor, but they are afraid of our whooping cough so we see them in the garden. We have pleasant friends among the soldiers, Major Edwards & others & we see Mr. Ward sometimes & Captain & Mrs. Bonvene.

On the 18th an eclipse of the sun. The light very fine. The sky blackish like a clear moonlight sky. The clouds wonderfully beautiful, dark towards the horizon, white higher except that now & then about the sun they are amber. The gulls fly slowly & heavily & there is a sleepy light over down & sea & cape.

28th. Ally reads me the greater part of a most interesting article in the *Quarterly* on The Book & its Mission. The Bradleys are here. After Edith & the boys' tea they play at the Emperor of Morocco & A. generally succeeds in making them laugh. They insist that Mr. Bradley & myself should play too, [we] acquit ourselves well.

29th. We write about the Franklin Epitaph. Aunt Franklin is about to sail for America.

August

5th. A. & the boys take me in my little carriage by the Wilderness, Abraham's Mead & Hill Close, up the Down by the green road & home by the steps A. made for me. They go over the stile & gather wild flowers with which I make a glorious bowl on our return. A delightful day—once more our wild gallop on the down but not alone this time for the boys are with us.

A. reads me some of Smiles' *Self-Help* & we resolve to get it for the boys.

6th. We put the beautiful Briary wreath which A. gathered for me yesterday on his chair & flowers around him with our little gifts—the boys' all—their sovereigns each in a purse. A peaceful day. A. in good spirits. Mrs. Cameron sends a copy of the beautiful Florentine Dante. Mr. White kindly comes from Bonchurch with Joliffe on some business matter . . .

[In London again, they visit the Alhambra, much taken with one of the horsemen, and Alfred accompanies Hallam to another treat, the Panorama of Venice. Alfred travels down to Cornwall – researching the *Idylls* – and on to the Isles of Scilly; 'he tells of hedges of scarlet Geranium, a delight to the eye & of Indian Aloes thirty feet high in flower which stand out all the winter & yet neither peach nor mulberry will ripen there'.]

September

16th. . . . We go home on the 22nd after having rested at Burlington House. The boys very pleased to get home in spite of all their late pleasures & indulgences. We see all our pleasant neighbours.

26th. A. arrives unexpectedly as I am dressing for dinner. He looks well & is very cheerful.

October

3rd. Poor Sir John Simeon's first visit after his wife's death. A sad day. He gives me her little garden chair. Edmund Lushington, Nanny & Agnes staying with us & Enid & Constance Guest often with us. Edmund & A. have good walks. We resume our old ways much to the boys' delight. I read about Galileo to them. A. reads me bits from the Laws of Howel Dda.

Mr. Cameron signs the agreement for Long's house the lease of which he buys.

Ally & the boys take me out in my little carriage & after dinner & tea he and I have long talks in the old way before we had so many guests. Sir John & Louy Simeon come to dinner. Pleasant to see him more himself & to have the old companionship with Louy. Madame Ernestina begs to read Ally's poems to him that she may have his opinion of her reading. She reads to him & he to her. I note she invents wonderful stories of her visit of three hours.

October. This month we are very busy heating the bath & the green house, settling about alterations in the Farm cottage, making the road of the hollow way, there being a right of foot path past our garden & park. We are thankful to have been allowed to put the road further off, we making it rather shorter than before. We see a good deal of Lady Charlotte & Mr. Schreiber & of Enid & Constance. Lady Charlotte tells me that of Cobden which makes me feel that I have misjudged him. The clergyman living near him says that he is a very good religious man, very sad from the loss of his sister.

November

1st. We hear of the wreck of a French sloop under our down. Ally takes me up the down, all the rest helping. Mr. Patmore who, poor man, is worn out by six months of night watching over his wife is with us.

Frederic & Guilio come. Captain Hamond tells us that Government is going to adopt his plan for the fortification of the Needles' end of the Island. He gives us an air plant brought by himself from America.

6th. A. reads 'Guinevere' to the Schreibers & Enid & Constance.

7th. Mr. Patmore goes, the better we hope for his visit. Mrs. Fox gives the boys Rifle caps & haversacks. We have them drilled by a soldier from the Fort. Happy days. A. wraps me in his waterproof & three doubles of fur besides & draws me about in my little carriage day by day, the boys helping.

22nd. The first trees felled for the road. We go to look at them. We pick the places for the bridge & the back gate. We look at the men sawing in a pit made of four crates, also at the wood fire in which the piles for the bridge are charred.

December

5th. I go thro' the new Back entrance, A. taking me in my little carriage with Heard's help. A. & I both think the road very picturesque. I go on the bridge which is almost finished, I believe, except the railings.

A poor ilex cut down. Necessary as its removal is if we would have sun one cannot but regret it.

19th. Mr. Palgrave comes. The road is opened. Mr. White & Mr. Joliffe here. Mr. Schreiber, Lady Charlotte, Miss Collyer, Mrs. Fox, Mr. Cotton & his sister in the evening. We play at 'Coach' & 'Earth, air & water'. Mr. Schreiber tells us of the quiet pony he has bought for us. This is their last evening. We could scarcely have had pleasanter neighbours. The boys write their thanks to Mr. Schreiber. We plan about the Coach house & cottages.

The Bridge and the Green Door behind Farringford

22nd. A. reads the poems to us chosen by Mr. Palgrave for his 'Golden Treasury'. I go out with A. to see which trees are to be cut down. A delightful gush of sunshine, when the tree whose shadow trembles on the wall, falls. 'Golden Treasury' these evenings.

29th. Mr. Palgrave goes. Charles Weld still with us. He tells us that at one time his brother had a fancy to have all he could made on his own estate and that delicious oil was made then from poppy seeds. The milk of the poppy, he said, turned black in an hour.

1861

January

1st. The day saddened by news of the death of the poor coastguard who trying to save something from a wreck was killed by a stone falling on his head while mounting one of the cliffs. But for this the day is happy & peaceful with A. & the children. The boys are enchanted with their pony. They take it out walking with them & feed it. In the evening 'The Magic Lantern' delights them.

3rd. The servants have a little dance. Their guests have not left before five & they say that they have been very happy, a pleasant thought for us. Weather cold & bright. The Bradleys here.

10th. Miss Watson, the old Somersby Governess, comes.

15th. Mr. Jowett comes having had to sleep at Lymington. When Miss Watson crossed the boat had to be cut out of the ice.

18th. Mr. Benson, the future Archbishop & his wife, come in the evening; Mr. & Mrs. Dobell & their friend Miss Jolly. The Bradleys & Miss Collyers dine with us. All our kind neighbours call. Mrs. Grosvenor Hood makes her little dog perform for the boys.

24th. Sir John Simeon, Louy & Dr. Logan meet the Bensons & Bradleys at dinner. Harriet [Cameron] is staying with us. A very pleasant evening.

29th. The Bradleys & Mr. Philpott, Mrs. Bradley's Father, dine with us.

31st. They go. A. & the boys help to make a window in the wall & A. takes me to see all that has been done & I like it much. We fix the line of the sunk fence. He reads to me 'The Ode on the Duke' & 'The Brook'.

February

2nd. Louy Simeon has been staying with us but leaves to-day. A. & the boys go with me to look at the work. I delighted with all that has been done.

4th, 5th, 6th. We [are] still looking after the work & finding it very satisfactory. He tells me his little song about the [illegible]* which he has just made. He writes it down and brings it to me in my room.

7th. I go out with A. before he leaves for Town about his teeth. We decide to have the Stables & Brew House pulled down, good tho' they are, but too near the house. Harriet [Cameron] goes with A. The house desolate as usual without him.

11th. The boys & I look after the works—the poor Brew House nearly down.

12th. Hallam & I watch the undermining of the Coach House wall with levers.

13th. A. returns so now we have him with us to watch the work.

17th. He tells me about his 'Northern Farmer'.

18th. He brings me down a blue-red book (welcome sight!) with part of it written down after he & the boys have worked at the bank of the hollow way, I putting a few spades full of sand on it.

19th. The boys watch our game of Backgammon & ask me to teach them. I read some of 'Sir Gareth' to the boys. Mr. Dakyns comes. Lionel wild with excitement. Delightful to find Mr. Dakyns so kind & pleasant & so intelligent looking. (Lionel makes what he calls a welcome to the Tutor which he means to sing, flag in hand, but his courage fails & he only puts snowdrops into Mr. Dakyn's room. He is most kind in working with us at digging sand. He takes the hardest part).

The boys walk with him & romp with him & on the 25th begin Lessons. I cannot but miss the life we have hitherto had however good I hope the change is in some way.

27th. Mr. Dakyns helps Ally & the boys with my little carriage & they rush along the road with me, a wild part, to call on the Cloughs

---

*Possibly referring to the 'Northern Farmer – Old Style', which the poet mentions on the 17th February.

& the Collyers. We generally have a little bit of Homer from A. in the evening and occasionally some of the Bible. Very delightful.

March

1st. The crocuses planted at last so we may hope for our golden ring. A. & I go round with Heard to see what shrubs can be moved to the bank. We have lost so many this winter that it is somewhat difficult to cover it even with help of a good many new ones. We watch the work unloading of the wagon which has brought them. Mr. Dakyns most unselfish & thoughtful for others. He helps us to plant the great Portugal laurel in the bank, the first tree there. Very pleasant to see the bank being clothed day by day more & more.

10th. A grand hailstorm. The boys watch it coming down with black fingers over the sea. A bright light behind. Something like that storm which A. & I saw over York plain as we stood on Richmond hill.

The Dean of Chichester arrives. The Cloughs come to us in the day time, he not being well enough to go out in the evening but he romps with the boys notwithstanding and helps to teach them chess. Florence dines with the boys in honour of our Lionel's birthday & before ours they & their children leave. Good indeed to have had such people as they & the Dean.

15th. The first flower on the bank to-day—a rose-coloured Rhododendron. Turfing begins on the lawn.

19th. Mr. Lear comes. He dines with us but too sad at the loss of the sister who has brought him up from his birth to stay with us altogether, so takes rooms at Murrow's, but he finds the society of the place too much for him & walks to Cowes on the 24th.

25th. Mr. Jowett comes. I ill in my room.

28th. A. takes me down for an hour after tea.

April

1st. Franklin Lushington comes. Always welcome. Mr. Clark arrives unexpectedly. Both pleased with the changes. The Feres & the Coltmans here & the Cloughs. The gentlemen dine with us, the ladies come in the evening.

8th. Mr. Jowett goes with the boys and myself to call on Mr. Bryce. Mr. Jowett takes lodgings at Dore's. A. puts me in a warm seat under the hedge that was, the mound belt that is & we watch the planting. Mr. Dakyns goes with him to Rogers's nursery gardens at Lymington for more plants. Heard with them. Day by day we watch the planting A. & I.

15th. Matilde arrives. A. reads 'Locksley Hall'.

18th. Some Hamlet and gets Matilde to read some Goethe & he reads some to her & she praises his reading very much & she is a lady of Saxony.

19th. He reads some of Shakespeare's sonnets. Our neighbours are so friendly as to take interest in the changes we have made & come to see them. Mr. Cotton says it is Fairyland. He has been so good as to send us things from Afton. Happy readings at night & pleasant talks. The boys bring us handfuls of flowers from the Rue.

No reading, we talk of Darwin.

23rd. Horatio & Charlie & their little Cecilia & Maud cross in a thunderstorm. A. & I superintend the planting of Butcher's broom & lilies. He & Mr. Dakyns go to hear a nightingale in the withy. Sergeant Keowen has been drilling the boys for some time past & they beg us to go & see their review. To our astonishment we find the Miss Collyers' carriage drawn up in Maiden's Croft & the Miss Collyers, the Miss Feres & Mrs. Cameron all gaily dressed. Charlie & Horatio also join us. In the afternoon A. takes me into the Conservatory & bids me ask Charles & Nanny & Agnes to come here until their new home Aubrey is ready. A moment not to be forgotten since I know that he longs to be alone. He & I out most days still looking after alterations in the garden. He finds the Butcher's cart overturned & the horse down, the horse having overreached itself in trying to get at grass on the bank. Mr. Isaacson helps to get them up.

May

9th. Kind letters about our going to Cambridge for his D.C.L. A. has had palpitation of the heart which prevents him from accepting it at once. We have been making the experiment of 'meaty tea' lately. Mr. Jowett kindly comes to it from time to time. He & Horatio teach the boys chess.

13th. Horatio & his go.

15th. It is decided that we do go to Cambridge & that we start to-morrow for Oatlands Park Hotel. Mr. Dakyns having kindly preceded us to find whether there are rooms. The situation of the Hotel delightful. A.'s heart is so bad when we are there that we telegraph to give up Cambridge. He takes me into the garden to see the beautiful banks of the river. In the evening he tells me that he is convinced smoking is the cause of the palpitation & that he resolved to leave it off. He takes his pipe up to the Belvedere, smokes it & breaks it & scatters the tobacco to the winds. We drive to St. George's Hill. A. & the boys walk over it & I wait for them. They return with handfuls of beautiful white narcissus with crimson-ringed caps. The boys take me to a great oak which A. has admired. A. walks to Hampton Court.

22nd. He takes the boys & myself to Winchester on our way home. The boat aground at Lymington but after some delay we get off. A letter from A. telling of his walk to the million butter-cupped churchyard where the faithful servants lie.

27th. He returns & tells me of the glowing feelings of health he has had in the mornings since he left off smoking & of his having been so hungry. We are out nearly all day looking after flower-beds. He takes my chair from place to place. I persuade him to go to Lyndhurst for walks in the forest, palpitation having somewhat returned.

The Welds & Edmund come.

June

4th. Edmund joins A. in the New Forest.

6th. They return.

8th. Edmund goes. We see two strange birds dark with light feathery tufts & a proud walk (probably Hoopoes).

Mr. Dakyns meets his friend Mr. Sedgewick who comes to tea.

12th. A swarm of bees in & about A.'s study window which we all go to watch.

13th. A. has hay fever or our wedding day would have been a happy one. Glorious sunshine. All this while whooping-cough has never left us. The doctor who sees Hallam says the cough is only from weakness & that the best possible thing will be to take him to the Pyrenees . . .

[The Tennysons set out for the Pyrenees, meeting Arthur Clough on the way. They are agreeably struck by the Cathedral at Bourges; 'its great pillars so beautiful in their simplicity almost took away one's breath with awe on first seeing them. The roof was flushed by the colours of the fine old windows'. The reasons for such reverent travel are touchingly laid bare by Emily in her description of their first view of the Pyrenees 'glorious with a sort of spiritual clearness and distinctness'. Such illumination feeds directly into poetry. 'But very pleasant it is to see Ally absorbed as he is by the beauty of the scene where the green Gave de Pau dashes by, breaking continually into little joyous looking fountains seeming fuller of life than any great rivers I ever saw. Alfred seems "as if possessed by the spirit of delight" amongst such scenery'.

The Tennysons travel back to the Isle of Wight via Paris – where the Louvre does not impress them – and Winchester, where the Cathedral does.]

September

How delightful to be at home once more. How beautiful it looks. It loses nothing in comparison with all we have seen. If A. were but well there would be nothing to be desired, but we suffer from the chill nights in the Pyrenees.

We find Mrs. Magendio[?] here & Lady Charlotte Schreiber, Enid & Constance & Blanche Guest with Miss Kemble besides all the dear old friends of the neighbourhood. We take to our new occupation of inspecting cows & horses & carts bought by the bailiff Heard in our absence as well as to the old ways.

October

11th. A very kind letter from Lord Dufferin of Ava . . . The tenant Merwood sends in the keys before twelve. The boys see the cows & sheep driven off the farm, the mast of the ship preceding. It makes one sad. Most changes do, I suppose. We are too late to see the sowing of the vetch. All the first seed sown.

17th. Mr. Cotton calls about Shakespeare's 'New Place' to be in the market to-morrow. Pleasant to see so thorough a country squire of the old stamp anxious to save it from desecrating hands. Mr. Peel with us these days.

19th. A happy old home day. A. & the boys take me about the fields in my little carriage. Mr. Dakyns with them. A. tells us his Ode for the Exhibition and reads us many Poems from the *Golden Treasury* in the evening.

20th. The boys take me to Maiden's Croft & we go to meet A. & Mr. Dakyns who are returning from the Needles. They tell me of the Military road which is being made to the old Light House. So the beautiful lonely down we shall see no more. I tell A. how much I have been interested by passages in Stanley's *Council of Nice.* He reads them to us & is as delighted as I was.

21st. A. tells me his 'Ode on the Exhibition' that I may write it down.

22nd. He reads to us the IVth Book of *Paradise Lost.*

28th. A. goes to Town for a doctor not having been well since our journey. I go to the boat with him. The ropes of boats get entangled in the wheel of the steamer. The Governor of the castle & the sailors are very kind in telling me about it & assuring me there is no danger. The sea is rough & I wait until the steamer appears well on its way. Franklin Lushington has been so kind as to lend A. his Chambers in the Temple & when he returns to them Mr. Venables lends his. The doctor says A. is below par. During his absence the boys sometimes amuse themselves with riding home on the Farm horses after their day's work and in driving home cows & in milking them. I read them Mr. Knowles's King Arthur stories in the evening which delight them greatly, also stories of India. Constance & Blanche Guest are often with the boys. I make manuscript books for A. & arrange his study. A. weary while A.'s absence has been. He returns on the 23rd of November, but he does not look as I would have him. He is pleased with all that has been done indoors & out of doors. A. reads some of Mr. Woolner's Journal to me.

November

28th. Dr. Acworth comes, talks about Homeopathy.

December

6th. He goes. A. has read to us these evenings. Dr. Acworth brought the account of the American insult making us of course extremely angry & Mr. Dakyns walks to Yarmouth for Papers.

11th. A. reads me what he has done of 'Enoch Arden'. Very fine & very beautiful it seems to me.

13th. Mr. Dakyns goes because his Father is so ill & A. helps me with the boys.

15th. A note from Blanche with Lady Charlotte's photograph. In it she tells the most sad news of the Prince Consort's death. A terrible blow. One fears for the Queen, for the nation, the loss is so unspeakable.

16th. We send for News from Yarmouth, we are so anxious about the Queen.

17th. A grand & touching account of the Queen.

20th. We learn to-day that the Queen arrived at Osborne yesterday. Not one even of her own servants on the platform only her children & Lord Alfred Paget.

22nd. A letter from Osborne.

23rd. The Prince's funeral day. A bitter east wind & dull sky.

24th. We go to Osborne, A., myself & the boys. We have a good report of the dear Queen & Princess Alice. A beautiful day. We find Mr. Palgrave arrived on our return.

27th. Kind Mr. Cotton offers to give £50 of the hundred which Starks asks for the road rather than have The Terrace spoilt. A. has walks with me or with Mr. Palgrave & the Bradleys & our boys.

1862

January

1st. A. walks with Mr. Palgrave & the boys and as Hallam says skips about like a young man.

2nd. Sir John Simeon brings his new wife.

7th. A. sends his 'Dedication' of his *Idylls* to the Duchess of Argyll & the Duchess of Sutherland. I think it magnificent. The boys busy writing what they call poems about the Prince.

9th. News that the Commissioners are to be given up, serves to make one thankful. Mr. Bradley brings Mr. Groves's interesting account of the Samaritan Day of Atonement. The boys listen with great pleasure to all of it that I have time to read to them. The boys delighted to hear that Mr. Dakyns will probably return to-day. They put up their flags & put on their rifle caps & receive him with military honours. A. reads to us at night. We learn that Lord Granville took the Ode on the Exhibition to the Queen when he went to Osborne for that first sad Privy Council & that the lines in it to the memory of the Prince should stand.

13th. A letter from the Duchess of Sutherland saying how much she likes the Dedication. We send it with a letter from A. to the Princess Alice. Also we send what, I suppose, will be the final form of the Ode to Sterndale Bennett.

16th. A day to be remembered by us. A letter of thanks to A. from Princess Alice telling us that his lines have soothed our Queen. Thank God! Also a very nice letter from Sir Charles Phipps. The guns firing this morning for the first time since the Queen said that they were not to fire again till further orders. Mr. Woolner comes.

17th. A. brings me violets, primroses, anemones.

21st. Snow over all. Frank's wedding day.

25th. Snow gone. A. & I walk these days & to-day I walk up the down with him, for the first time for years. Very beautiful. Mr. Dakyns kindly runs back for the little carriage & they take me to the beacon.

27th. Dr. Sterndale Bennett comes.

28th. He goes & Mr. Jowett arrives. The boys delighted [to] drive to meet him. His cough too bad to read them Homer as usual but he plays at chess with them & we played 'Proverbs' in the evening. Jeffrey's photographs come.

31st. To-day he must go. Every day I have had interesting talks with him.

February

1st. A. reads us what he has done of 'Enoch Arden'. Very beautiful & heroic, I think it. A. reads us some of Jacob & Esau & other parts of the Old Testament & the boys interested by the death of Polycarp in Miss Sewell's *Church History* . . .

3rd. A. reads the first of the *Nights on the Goodwin Sands* in 'Macmillan'. A true story of wonderful heroism.

4th. He takes me to see the snowdrops which seem to us to have a peculiar beauty & whiteness this year. First snowdrops. He reads us the second Ramsgate lifeboats Paper this evening. Noble fellows!

6th. Parliament meets. Lord Dufferin quotes the end of A.'s 'Dedication'. Dr. Latham comes. His talk very clever & learned, moreover. A. looks for an umbrella to shelter me from the East wind & paints the gate green to please me.

7th. We are inexpressibly vexed to see a paragraph in the *Daily Telegraph* speaking of the letter from Princess Alice & cannot think who has been so ill-judged as to put it in. A. writes to Mr. Dasent to prevent it from slipping into the *Times.*

21st. A. & Mr. Dakyns have played several evenings at Backgammon & sometimes I play meanwhile on the piano.

23rd. A. reads us some of 'Enoch Arden' to my delight & begins writing it down regularly to-day.

24th. We were to have gone to Shiplake to-day to have said good-bye to the place where we were married, but East wind & mist & rain prevented us. An extremely interesting letter from the Duke of Argyll with a most touching message from the Queen. Also a deeply moving half letter, half thinking on paper, from the Princess Royal. One cannot but feel an added glow of devotion to them seeing how anxious they are to thank A. A day I would fain remember for more even than that or even this—that I have read what A. has written of 'Enoch Arden' this morning.

25th. Sir John Simeon calls. A. writes to the Princess & copies for her 'The Passing of Arthur'.

26th. He goes to Shiplake. A sharp bitter East wind. He will not hear of my exposing myself to it. I read some Mill & Sir Alexander Grant's Lecture on the Roman colonies.

March

1st. A few lines from Kate telling that A. is coming home. She thinks him looking as young or younger than when we married. He looks well on his return. Another extremely interesting letter from the Duke of Argyll.

2nd. A. reads 'The Parting Hour' to us.

4th. We meet Sir A. Sterling & Mr. Stirling of Kier at Swainston. All very kind & pleasant but I find it hard work to leave home even for a night.

5th. See the dear little faces watching the return.

9th. A. walks for a hour at night with Mr. Dakyns.

13th. The Duke & Duchess of Argyll come to us. Lord Dufferin does not arrive. A. reads 'Enoch Arden' to us.

14th. The poor Duke & Duchess kept in doors from bad colds. Lord Dufferin arrives after an adventurous journey accomplished as far as Cowes before breakfast. A. reads 'Enoch Arden' to him. The boys enchanted with the Wilson's tales.

15th. They must all leave to-day. One has learned to love the Duke & Duchess & Lord Dufferin is delightful.

16th. Our Lionel's birthday. He delighted with a knife & both boys very pleased with their Peter the Whaler, Parker's Church stories, African Wanderers, Mère Angelique.

The most absolute regularity & quiet home ways seem necessary to A. now. Read Lord Dufferin's very interesting book.

25th. A letter from the Duke & Duchess of Argyll giving A. the Queen's Command to go to Osborne.

31st. Mr. Spedding sends us his *Bacon's Life & Letters.*

April

4th. Mr. Atkinson comes.

6th. Mr. King comes.

9th. Sir John Simeon comes from Town, dines & sleeps here. Wins Mr. Atkinson's heart as he does most hearts.

10th. Mr. Warburton arrives . . .

11th. A letter from Colonel Biddulph fixing Monday at 3 p.m. for his visit.

12th. Mr. Dakyns & the boys meet Mr. Jowett.

14th. Mr. Jowett kindly accompanies A. in his drive to Osborne, my cough being bad. A. affected even to tears by the Queen, who stood pale & statue-like, speaking in a quiet, sweet, sad voice. She looked very pretty and had a stately innocence about her different from other women. She said many kind things to him, for he remem-

Alfred Tennyson, photographed at Manchester by James Mudd, *c.* 1860

From the Tennyson Research Centre Collection, Lincoln, by courtesy of Lord Tennyson and Lincolnshire Library Service

Alfred Lord Tennyson, Hallam and Lionel, photographed by Rejlander, *c.* 1862

From the Tennyson Research Centre Collection, Lincoln, by courtesy of Lord Tennyson and Lincolnshire Library Service

bers thanking her & saying that it made him very happy, but he does not remember what she said. She talked of the Prince & of Hallam & Macaulay & Göethe & Schiller in connection with him and said that the Prince was so like the picture of Arthur Hallam in *In Memoriam* even to his blue eyes, and when A. said he would have made a great King, she said, 'He always said it did not signify whether He did the right thing or did not so long as the right thing was *done'*. Ally said we all grieved with your Majesty & the Queen replied: 'The country has been kind to me & I am thankful'. Princess Alice came in with Princess Beatrice when the Queen had withdrawn and was very kind 'true natural & true mannered' as A. says.

The Henry Taylors & their daughters & Mr. Dodgson here at this time & we see them often.

16th. Mr. Dakyns goes. A sorrowful parting for all.

17th. Mr. Atkinson arrives. Mr. Jowett goes to the Terrace, three young friends with him.

21st. Nanny & Agnes arrive while the boys are walking with Mr. Jowett. Infinite joy at the meeting. The three young creatures give us Tableaux Vivants from Shakespeare & the Sleeping Beauty & Hallam gives up his part to Lionel in the sleepwalking scene in *Macbeth.*

23rd. Sterndale Bennett's setting of the 'Ode' arrives & Nanny gives it to us.

24th. I [play?] a little of it to Mr. Jowett.

25th. I go with A. to Yarmouth on his way to London. Lionel quite indignant with Nanny when she spoke of Mr. Jowett's 'pupils'. 'They are not his pupils at all. Mr. Jowett is a young lad. They are all just the same, just entering life together'. Mr. Jowett reads Homer to the boys & Agnes.

May

1st. A. splendid day for the opening of the Exhibition. I am sorry A. is not there but he would not, of course, join the Procession, nor did I wish him.

2nd. A. goes to Cliveden to-day.

3rd. Keeping shows his fossils to Nanny & the children. They are highly delighted. I buy one of the Collections he had made of the rocks of this part. The children very anxious to hear the 'Ode'. It is promised them after dinner. When we arrive in the drawing room, the shutters are drawn & the curtains. When undrawn they appear, the boys in nightdresses, Agnes also in white, over their dresses, they thinking so to do honour to the 'Ode' as 'choristers'. We do not know what to do for laughter.

7th. A. returns to-day. He has enjoyed his visit at Cliveden very much. He is very pleased to have met Mr. Charles Howard again & to have seen so much of Mr. Gladstone. He admires Lady Constance Grosvenor extremely & likes Lady Taunton very much. He brings a Wellingtonia, the gift of the Duchess. The seed was shot from a tree in California at two hundred feet from the ground. A. looks thin, but well & cheerful tho' he says he has had a touch of hay-fever. He & I look about the progress made in out of doors work & rejoice in the blossoming trees & flowery fields.

13th. A. brings down 'A Dedication'. I send it to the Publishers. These days he takes me delightful rounds in my little carriage.

14th. A letter from Mr. Jowett full of affectionate warning about my health to which A. bids me attend. He has for some time been talking of trying France & Germany again.

18th. He reads me one of Robertson's Sermons, 'Thus saith the High God'.

20th. A. mows, the boys sweep & I help a little.

23rd. We show Heard where we wish the Greenhouse flowers to be planted.

31st. A very interesting letter from Lady Augusta Bruce saying that she was commanded by the Queen to send A. two volumes of Poems by Zeller & another in which HM had found comfort. They are marked by herself. A precious gift. We finished *Robinson Crusoe.* Homages from Frenchmen to-day & four or five times lately. One is glad to have them.

June

5th. An Illustrated Edition of Gray with a kind note from Lady Taunton.

11th. I begin my rides on Fanny, A. walking by my side. Very pleasant.

12th. A. calls on Henry Taylor & Mrs. Cameron makes him read 'The Vision of Sin'.

13th. We keep our wedding secretly. A. does not like anniversaries & this one seems too sacred to keep openly.

14th. Henry Taylor, Mrs. Cameron & the Jacksons dine with us. A. reads 'Enoch Arden'. A very pleasant evening but that Mrs. Jackson was overpowered by 'Enoch Arden'. Her two dream girls haunt one. They seem to come out of some Niebelungenlied [German epic; 12th-13th century].

17th. A magnificent Blotting book from the manufacturers at Coventry with The Lady Godiva woven in silk.

18th. Mrs. Norton & Mr. Stirling of Kier call & walk with me & then call on Henry Taylor & Mrs. Cameron to return to dinner & drive back to Cowes after. Both very agreeable.

21st. Mr. Woolner comes. A. makes hay. I help a little.

30th. A. again out in the hay field at work nearly all day.

July

1st. The last load home to-night. A. helps to the last. Mrs. Cameron comes across the Park looking gorgeous in her violet dress & red cloak walking over the newly mown grass. Pleasant to hear the men cheering.

2nd. The Men's Festival Day.

3rd. Very sad account of the Patmores. The boys drill continually sometimes on foot, sometimes on pony back & on great days have reviews.

10th. Mr. Warburton dines with us.

12th. Frederick comes. Very pleased with what we have done in the grounds.

18th. Mr. & Mrs. Cameron have kindly lent us Ashburton Cottage & we go there with our boys . . .

[The Tennysons travel to London, where they are photographed by W. Jeffrey. Together they visit Newcastle – where 'the beautiful church near the market place gives the look of a foreign town' – and Lincoln Cathedral. Alfred tours Derbyshire and Yorkshire, while Emily visits her father at Grasby.]

September

13th. The roughest crossing we ever had. The old life, drills, walks, letters innumerable, & farm accounts. We look at pretty 'Nelly' with the Deer-like head, down sheep & a great many things besides. The boys like to read all about Garibaldi & Lionel wants to write to him & ask him here. A great noise among the Rooks. Mr. Atkinson & the boys have seen them chasing a Hawk these two or three days.

28th. A letter from Mr. Palgrave telling of his engagement. We are delighted to receive it.

29th. A. comes to show me a glorious rainbow. The whole arch, part of it is afterwards in a red sky, a sort of glorified rainbow, & then purple clouds float over it.

October

A. goes to Swainston, returns on the 16th with Mr. Woolner.

18th. Edmund comes. Very stormy. Two shipwrecks to-night. Edmund leaves on the 22nd in spite of storm & wind, the boatmen foretelling still worse to-morrow.

26th. A. calls on Mr. Ward at night. One day A. goes with me to see sheep marked. One [day] he piles up mangold wurzels.

30th. A. so good as to write to Mr. Gladstone & send what I want to have shown to him.

31st. A. on the platform watching the stars.

November

1st. Mr. Atkinson walks to Ventnor to see his friend Mr. Lubbock having heard of the death of his daughter.

7th. A very kind letter from Mr. Gladstone.

8th. Dr. Ogle dines with us.

9th. Rainy. We cannot go to church. A. reads the Bible to us in the evening.

10th. The boys make a bonfire in honour of Grandpapa's birthday. Hallam goes to the Ford with *In Memoriam* & the *Idylls* as a gift because Keown asked to have them lent to him because we hear that

Admiral Crozier is Lord of the Fleet. We go to the Admiral's. A. and I take Hallam.

13th. A calm, bright frost, air delicious. At night A. goes out on the platform to see if there are any shooting stars & has just said to himself, I must take care I do not fall, it is so dark, when he did fall over & cracked one of the glasses of his spectacles but did no harm to himself except a little scratch on his nose.

14th. We go to Coomb Bute where they are ploughing.

17th. A. has to go to Town to have a tooth stopt.

21st. Mr. Watts most kindly begins a portrait of me to surprise A. Mr. Watts so pleasant that the time does not seem long.

22nd. The boys so much interested in watching him that they beg not to go out. A. has to land in a little boat. A large Conger Eel at the landing place. I send the boys to look at it. A. brings me two Pompeian vases & one with a lizard. From Mr. Woolner a Fern dish.

27th. A. writes to thank Mr. Keeping for the curious Pewter fork & spoon which he found embedded in sand & shingle at Atherfield point & which he has given to A.

29th. Mr. Watts finishes my portrait to-day & begins one of A. Mr. Watts lunches with us & praises our bread. After luncheon Hallam takes a big loaf to him. Miss Thackeray is at the Camerons these days & we see her from time to time. A. has walked along the shore to Brixton [Brighstone].

December

1st. His portrait grows very grand to-day. Mr. Watts takes his little bit of bread & cheese with us again to-day. A. writes to Sir Redmond Barry to thank him for the Exhibition catalogue & the seeds of Wattle & the magnificent maize & the Victorian wheat & oats beautiful to behold. A. says that the oats look like stately Virgins the colour and shapes are so beautiful. We go to see the wheat sown.

3rd. Prince Alfred proclaimed King of Greece. Lionel has begun to learn Greek every day for most days.

4th. A. walks with Mr. Atkinson on Afton Down & reads in the moonlight.

16th. We plant roses. Mr. Routledge comes about the *Illustrated Edition of* the Poems.

18th. To my great delight A. begins reading Carlyle's 3rd vol. of *Frederich* & says he will read it to me. A return to our dear old ways most welcome to me.

19th. We are all out transplanting Rhododendrons, we choosing places, the boys helping to dig.

21st. A. reads me some of Horte's Thomas à Becket.

24th. Hallam puts up A.'s Holly wreath while we are at dinner. The boys have the Magic Lantern after having been to the accustomed house with gifts. I have a pleasant evening A. reading to me part of *King Lear* & put the gifts from Uncle & Aunt Charley & Grandpapa & ourselves by the sides of the boy's beds.

25th. A. reads me what he has done of the New Poem.

26th. Sir Graham Hamond's funeral day.

31st. All these days we have been planting.

1863

January

1st. Old Brian lunches here. Yesterday he walked from Newport, to-day he is going to Yarmouth & to-morrow back to Newport. He was ninety last Easter. Almost every evening A. reads *Friedrich* to me & everyday we are planting.

On the 3rd Euonymous in the glen.

4th. Every night A. reads some of Stanley's *Jewish Church** to me. Very interesting to both of us. In the morning we go out to look after the work going on in the grounds. In the afternoons letters & bills.

9th. Mr. & Mrs. Palgrave come to-day.

10th. Mr. Clark to-day. Mrs. Palgrave gives us Mozart & Beethoven in the evenings.

13th. All our pleasant guests go. We rejoice that Mr. Palgrave has a wife who seems so well fitted to make him happy.

---

*Arthur Penrhyn Stanley (1815-1881) published *History of the Jewish Church* in 1863 and 1865.

14th. A beautiful day. Lady Augusta Bruce comes to luncheon & brings with her what is to us beyond price *The Prince Consort,* a gift from the Queen with kind words written by H.M.'s own hand, also a beautiful photograph of herself & three of her children with A.'s lines under it 'May all love etc.' Also the prayers used at the Anniversary & the Sermon preached. I feel to know & to trust Lady Augusta at once. She promises to come & sleep here next week if she can.

15th. Rogers brings us two wonderfully beautiful numbers of Gould's *British Birds.*

17th. The boys go to meet Mr. Jowett.

19th. A delightful talk with him.

All Saints Church, Freshwater

20th. He & A. walk and the boys & I go to meet Mr. Dakyns. A. reads 'Enoch Arden' one evening and 'The Tapestried Chamber'. Mrs. Brookfield & Arthur here, also Sir Charles Darling.

February

13th. All this time planting goes on & alteration in the grounds & filling up the space left by the great Elm Tree to the South which we had to cut down, dear as it was, sunshine being dearer. To-day A. & the boys take me to the Terrace that we may plan the grounds there. Heard's brother who has been a sailor for twenty years says that he has never known so stormy a time as two months of this winter.

15th. A. brings me *The Times* to see the article on Mr. Jowett. Such a one as should be.

17th. A splendid day. A. went with Mr. Estcourt, Mr. Bird, Farmer Lane & Heard to walk the bounds of our Manor. A. reads me a little of Russell's Diary & one night he reads Virgil with me. Mr. Atkinson very kind in bringing barrows full of Ferns & primroses. The boys help, A. & I help them to plant.

24th. Mr. Cotton calls to make arrangements about the celebration of the Prince's Wedding day. We joyfully consent to having a Bonfire on our Down.

March

3rd. A. & Mr. Atkinson go with Keeping to Hampstead. The boys much interested by the specimens they bring home.

6th. We send off the final copy of 'A Welcome'.

7th. This has been a very busy week of preparations for the 10th even in this little place, making flags, planting flags, making favours, puddings, cakes & not only in our house but others also.

10th. A fine morning. A letter from Lady Augusta with a very kind message from the Queen about the 'Welcome' which arrived just after the Princess. We thought it would have arrived before. Poor A'.s ticket for the Chapel only arrives this morning having been missent so he misses the glorious pageant. I go with the boys & Mr. Atkinson to see the dinner. The sight of so many dear old gray heads is touching. The boys bring their beautiful Danish & English flags & walk in procession with the school children. The poor little fellows very much excited. Mr. Atkinson makes the flower vases beautiful. We dine in the nursery, all the down-stairs rooms being prepared for the evening. The Cake is lovely thanks to Andrews & Acott & Matilda. The supper too all we could wish adorned with flowers & the little flags painted by Mr. Atkinson & the boys. All our friends go on the Down with A. in spite of rain except Mr. & Mrs. Isaacson & Admiral Crozier. I go to the summer house in the kitchen garden with Mr. & Mrs. Isaacson & am joined by others.

A. tells me that the bonfire is very grand, great green tongues of flame dart out along the ground, curling & licking. The torchlight procession, too, very fine. The boys wait on us at supper. They want to stay up & drink the Queen's health & that of the Prince & Princess.

Of the Queen A. says the simple words 'The Queen & God bless her' very grandly & very impressively. There is a little dance after supper. The house looks very pretty with all the lamps & candles.

11th. Mrs. Gatty & her son Stephen come.

12th, 13th, 14th. They gather sea-weed.

16th. A. & I go to Osborne & write our names. We are much amused on returning to find that our neighbours have been drawn up in their carriages at our gate insisting that the Prince & Princess had promised a visit to-day or to-morrow & would not go until Mr. Atkinson assured them he knew nothing of it.

18th. Ellen & Zilly Lushington come. They have expeditions with A. & the boys.

23rd. Elizabeth and her husband leave. — Poor Lionel very sad.

27th. Nelly & Zilly go. Most glad we are to have had them. A. reads me some Comte. Dreary reading.

28th. Carpenter & Westley send us the account of their birthday Illuminations which excited so much interest especially that of The Prince Consort with A.'s lines 'O silent father of our Kings to be, Mourned in this [golden] hour of jubilee' on a . . . blue ground with gold & white clouds & a starry crown. A. reads me some *Othello.*

29th. To-day his own beautiful poem. A great refreshment.

30th. More *Othello.* Delightful to have our readings again.

31st. The boys go with me to meet Mr. Jowett. A. goes on with *Othello.*

April

1st. Charles Weld comes with the beautiful Urn & Salver graceful in form & design, we think, with a very kind inscription presented to A. in acknowledgement of the Ode on the Exhibition.

2nd. Mr. Jowett goes to the Terrace. Mr. Clark is with the Bradleys & they all dine with us.

10th. A. reads 'Aylmer's Field' to Mr. Jowett & me . . .

11th. Our London library books come. A. shows me the Pitcher Plant and reads me some of St. John's *Borneo**.

18th. Mr. Atkinson returns from his holiday & A. takes him at night

---

*S. St John, *Life in the Forests of the Far East,* 2 vols (1862).

to the rooms we have furnished for him [at] the Lodge. A. says that they look so delightfully comfortable, he would like to live there himself.

20th. A. & I find a person dressed as a gentleman squatting on the top of the bank & peering into our lawn. A. goes up to him and lets him come down. He says 'I hope you will forgive me, Mr. Tennyson'. A. replies, 'It is not pretty' & turns his back on him.

22nd. The Peregrine Falcons taken from our cliff have grown so tame that they will feed from Mr. Rogers' hand. At first the male used to stamp with rage & the female kept up a melancholy flapping of the wings & trod to death her little one hatched in captivity. The boys want to pay their five guineas for them & set them free. A. says it is useless, they would be taken again immediately or shot. Afterwards agrees to buy if the Maharajah to whom they are going finds them too much injured for use.

23rd. A Roman Urn found in the Terrace grounds when they were digging out earth for a mound. A. & I make out some of the thirty tyrants in Gaul of whose date the coins are. Near them was the skeleton of a horse's head in a circle of stones.

24th. Lord & Lady Lilford call with Mrs. Cameron, their little boy with them.

25th. They dine with us and Lord Lilford sings some very pretty Spanish and Greek songs.

May

1st. It is settled that Lord Lilford & A. go to the New Forest together. Meanwhile Rejlander, the Swedish photographer, has been making photographs of some of us. Lionel's very fine, A.'s profile good. He is still at his work when the gentlemen return from the Forest on the 5th, Kate & Drummond with them. The boys like his Norse tales.

9th. They go by the early [*sic*] & A. the boys & myself to Osborne. We lunch with Lady Augusta Bruce & afterwards drive with her in the grounds. We see the dairy. Very pretty it is lined with white Dutch tiles with a wreath of convolvulus round & a fountain in the middle, then the kitchen where the princesses amuse themselves with cooking, also lined with white tiles, the little garden, the fort which Prince Arthur has made, the pet donkey that draws the Gun carriage, the Swiss Cottage where they have their Museum and another where they come to tea. Soon after we return Lady Augusta is sent for & she comes to fetch us to the Queen. We wait in the Drawing-room & after a very little time we heard a quiet, shy opening of the door & the Queen came in & I kissed her hand. She shook hands with the boys & made a very low reverence to A. All the Princesses came in by turns. Prince Leopold also. All shook hands very kindly with us all. We had met Prince Alfred before in one of the corridors with Prince Louis of Hesse & he had shaken hands with A. & talked to him.

The Queen's face is beautiful. Not the least like her portraits but small & child-like, full of intelligence & ineffably sweet & of a sad sympathy.

A. was delighted with the breadth & freedom & penetration of her mind. One felt that no false thing could stand before her. We talked of all things in heaven & earth it seemed to me. I never met a Lady with whom I could talk so easily & never felt so little shy with any stranger after the first few minutes.

She laughed heartily at many things that were said but shades of pain & sadness passed over a face that seemed sometimes all one smile. Princess Alice joined pleasantly in the conversation. Prince Leopold & Lady Augusta talked with the boys.

One feels that the Queen is a woman to live and die for.

I am sorry that A. might not have a warm shake of the hand such as the boys & myself had when the Queen retired. I gave Princess Beatrice A.'s poems because she had said to Lady Augusta that she wished A. would write her some 'poetries' that she might learn when she was a big girl. A. wrote his name in the book & the Princess's. He & the boys had some tea & Lady Augusta went off with the Queen & Princess Alice to Newport. We saw them from a balcony when they drove away. A footman came to take us on the Terrace. As A. said the grounds looked sad, the hands that had laid them out being gone.

10th. Lord Lilford calls to say good bye.

11th. A Queen's messenger comes with Guizot's translation (made by order) of Prince Albert's speeches & *The Meditations* from the German with an Album of the Queen's in which A. is to write something. He writes 'All along the Valley'.

Letters from Lady Augusta to us both.

12th. A. finds me with a volume of Goethe looking for 'Edel sei der Mensch' & he reads this & other things to me.

13th. He tells me what Tyndall says of the sun as the fountain of our heat & motion. We see Lady Lilford these days.

18th. On the 18th she goes & Mr. Spring-Rice & Ailene come. Mr. Venables expected but does not arrive.

19th. We are all vaccinated including Ailene. She sings Hayden's beautiful Cazonet of 'Good Morrow'.

21st. A.'s dear old friend Spring-Rice & his Ailene go to-day. They have had rainy, stormy weather while with us, alas!

22nd. The butterfly which Rogers sent in the chrysalis that A. might see it emerge comes out unperceived. A. fetches me that I may see it. I find it standing on the chrysalis.

25th. Mr. Venables comes.

27th. Mr. Lefroy & Emma & Nanny & Agnes also come & Sir John & Louy Simeon. We have a very pleasant evening.

29th. Mr. Venables goes. Mr. Lefroy & Emma next day.

31st. Lord Somers dines with us and interests us much by his talk of many lands & many things.

Mr. & Mrs. Pike call in the morning. He is United States minister at the Hague.

June

11th. Mr. Moncure Conway comes on a mission from America.

12th. He lunches with us. He interests us. He has released his Father's slaves & tells us that in no instance have they failed, but have uniformly turned out well, working well & making for themselves a good position tho' he could only afford to give them a roof over their heads & a very little to start with. He says that not one of the West Indian islands accepted the Government offer except Antigua & that this is why emancipation has failed in all the other islands, the slaves not having been freed at once as in Antigua . . .

20th. Some unknown friend sends A. Colenso's work*.

22nd. The Duke & Duchess of Argyll come. They admire the gardens & the farm. A. reads 'Aylmer's Field'.

23rd. They go with A. to Hampstead. under Keeping's escort. A. reads 'Boädicea' & 'The Bugle Song'.

---

*John William Colenso (1814-1883), Bishop of Natal; published a series of treatises on the Pentateuch between 1862 and 1879.

24th. The Duke & Duchess with A. & the boys who bring back the Duchess as she cannot go up the Down. The Duke delighted with it. We all sit in the new lawn & then they must go. Very good in them to have come so far for such a little time. The Duke sees a Kestrel fly past with a bird & finds the nest of a golden crested wren in the Arbor Vitae. While they are with us Watt's portrait of me comes. They all say it is a Gainsborough.

25th. A. was to have gone to Little Holland House, breakfasted at Argyll Lodge to-morrow to meet Sir John Lawrence & Mr. Clark but Edmund writes to say that he is coming so A. stays to see him & goes on the 27th. He sees doctors for a gouty affliction.

Paget says it only needs patience cure.

July

11th. Cissy & Lucy come & Edmund walks to meet them.

12th. A. goes to Mr. Palgrave's. Every one most kind to him. The weather sunny & beautiful & Edmund, Cissy say that they enjoy themselves.

23rd, 24th, 25th, 26th. Days of trouble & anxiety & preparation. A. is advised by the doctors not to return home at present. We go to join him in Town & travel with Edmund & Cissy. We stay at Lansdowne Crescent & see A. from time to time . . .

[A. visits doctors in London about his gout, which Sir James Paget – the most renowned pathologist of the day – says 'only needs patience cure'. He certainly feels better for a visit to York, where he tours the cathedral. Back in London, there is a more serious threat to health, when the cab in which the whole family is travelling overturns. 'The poor horse was perfectly quiet or we must have been smashed to pieces'.]

September

14th. We set off home & reached it after a good journey. To my great delight & thankfulness, A. is pleased with the alterations I have had made during his absence and immediately orders the completion of my plan. I find a beautiful oak desk, Edmund's birthday gift to me made by Frank's direction & suggested by my Hallam. Edmund is here, Nelly and Emmy also.

16th. Frank & Kate & their baby are also here. The Pollocks, Mrs. Clough & the Coltmans here. We see all from time to time. Mr. Clifford, Louy Simeon and her friend.

We have had earth from the Prince's Bonfire put in the yard that flowers may grow!

October

We have been watching the growth of the Fernery which we are putting just beyond where the great black wooden doors into the yard used to be. The soil is from Headon Hill. A box from Coniston with Stag's Horn moss & grass of Parnassus for which we have asked. We go on with planting different things as usual.

10th. Mr. Butterworth goes. Miss Perry, Mr. Donne, Mr. & Mrs. King. She very charming. She tells me of the letter she has had from Garibaldi in consequence of her poem on Aspromonte.

17th. The boys go to Colwell Bay to wave a flag as the *Tasmania* passes; William Seaton having left us to be Steward on board. They see two pocket handkerchiefs waving on deck. A. is reading me Andrea in the evenings and some of Stanley's *Jewish Church.* A. very successful in mending a broken vase & other things with Underwood's cement. He & the boys & Henry Cameron take me up the down in my little [carriage] & come by the green road, then walk up the steps with Ally which he has made for me.

A. reads some Virgil with me. Hallam enjoys translating his Virgil & Lionel his Horace. They are reading Cave Brown's *Siege of Delhi* which I have just read with great interest & they both enjoy Agnes Strickland in the evening reading. I am happy teaching them. (What a pity this cannot last). Hallam finishes the end book of the *Aeneid.* Lionel likes learning these Odes of Horace.

28th. A. reads me his magnificent sermon in 'Aylmer's Field'.

November

2nd. A. reads me some of Coleridge's poems.

6th. Some of his (Dry Bones poem) ['Aylmer's Field'].

7th. Some of Edward's Captivity in Poland. Extremely interesting.

8th. We read Manzoni's magnificent ode 'Egli fù' & Gladstone's &

Goethe's translation. A. walks most mornings with both the boys now & they all take me in my little carriage as usual.

11th & 14th. A. busy with his translation of Homer. We hear from the Duchess of Argyll and Mr. Jowett about Lady Augusta's marriage to Dr. Stanley.

16th. A. shows me his Alcaics [classical metre].

17th. He helps me with Hallam's lessons because he saw I was so tired yesterday. While we are planting trees we hear almost daily of other people building houses here.

25th. A. reads his 'Aylmer's Field' to me which seems to me very beautiful tho' we neither of us much like the story.

26th. Mr. Wilson recommended by Mr. Clark comes. A. reads something from the *Cornhill* to us. They with the boys take me to the Beacon in my little carriage & run all the way from the beacon to the ledge back.

30th. A photograph from Cincinnati of Donaldson's Lotos Eaters comes. A pleasant picture but not A.'s.

December

1st. We hear that Mr. Bradley is very pleased with A.'s 'bits of Homer, the only perfect reproduction of the passage', to which A. replies 'not perfect'.

2nd. Sir John & Lady Simeon dine with us. A. reads his 'Northern Farmer' & that wonderful prophecy in the Polish Captivity.

5th. I busy copying out the first word of every line of 'Enoch Arden' because A. thinks of sending it to be published for a Christmas book, & he has no other copy, and we fear that this may be lost.

8th. A. reads some of the Cabbala [Hebrew tradition] to us.

17th. A. reads to me 'Edel sei der Mensch' & other poems of Goethe & Fitzgerald's translation of *Omar Khayyám* [Persian poet, 1048-1131].

21st. A. reads Milton & some of the Bible to us.

22nd. Lady Augusta's wedding day. The boys hoist flags & fire caps in honour. From the Bradleys we have an interesting account of the wedding which was by torchlight in Westminster Abbey & very imposing.

Mr. Palgrave is with us. Mr. & Mrs. Butler in lodgings.

25th. Today we hear of Mr. Thackeray's death. A great shock.

26th. Mr. Allingham comes so we have a pleasant party & A. has good walks with Mr. Bradley & Mr. Butler. One day Mr. Butler brings his big dog Nelson which puts his paws round me & fondles my arm & is most affectionate to Lionel.

1864

January

4th. A. & I call on the Miss Thackerays. Hallam takes me in the little carriage.

13th. Mr. Dakyns arrives. The boys wild with delight tumbling over one another all the afternoon.

17th. A. & I walk thro' Maiden's Croft to Hill Close to see it now that the hedge is thrown down between the two trees. — We like it. We never tire of the fields. A. reads of the Schism between the early Weston Church in Nordheim*.

20th. The Bradleys go but Mr. Philpott remains & A. has some walks with him.

February

2nd. A. reads me some of his little poem. A meteor falls & burst into sparks midway from the zenith just over the wreath of elms.

3rd. A. is writing out his small poems. A letter from the Dean of Windsor saying that the Queen would be very much pleased if A. would write four lines to be put on the statue of the Duchess of Kent in the Frogmore Mausoleum. A. sends four lines.

A letter from Mrs. Bruce saying that beautiful as they are they are not what the Queen wants.

A. sends several forms of lines. The Dean had not explained the Queen's idea. Most gracious & kind thanks from the Queen thro' Mrs. Bruce who tells us that one form is already in the sculptor's hands.

---

*Nordheim was a town a few miles south-east of Minden in old Saxony where Otto ruled and died in 1083. His enemy, King Henry IV, was excommunicated in 1076 by the Pope.

Freshwater Bay and the waves that sound like a 'broad-flung ship-wrecking roar'
photo R.J.H.

A view from the foot of Tennyson Down of the track made for the Tennysons from the back gate of Farringford.
Maiden's Croft is on the left with the 'wilderness' in the background *photo R.J.H.*

St. Agnes' thatch-roofed church, Freshwater Bay. *photo R.J.H.*
The land on which it stands was donated by the Tennysons

The grave of Emily Tennyson (right) and the family tomb (centre)
in All Saints' churchyard, Freshwater *photo R.J.H.*

7th. A. scrambles with the boys & Mr. Wilson by the cliffs from Watcombe Bay to Freshwater. He reads a sermon to us in the evening.

8th. Goes to town to-day.

10th. A letter telling that he is all safe at Mr. Spedding's rooms.

13th. A letter from A. with 'Enoch Arden' printed.

14th. To-day his letter comes with 'Aylmer's Field', 'Sea Dreams', & 'The Grandmother'.

15th. Nanny and Agnes come and bring me an 'Illustrated News' with a portrait of A. Not bad and a kind of appreciative memoir.

16th. Mr. Chapman sends me a copy by A.'s request.

March

1st. A beautiful day to welcome him. We all go to meet A. How long it seems since he left me! He interests us all very much in the evening. He shows me his sheets and reads the 'Northern Farmer' to Nanny & wants her to stay longer but she must not disappoint the sisters at Bath. Heard & Mr. Wilson look about Aubrey for her.

2nd. A. & I talk about the poems in the evening after Hallam has read one of the leading articles of the day to us.

5th. Plays a little at football.

9th, 10th, 11th, 12th. Mr. Wilson & I play at Backgammon in the evenings with A.

15th. A. laying down turf. Mr. Wilson helps.

16th. Lionel gets up at half past twelve to look at his birthday gifts. He rides with his gifts to different cottages on the down, his cap blows off & frightens Fanny & he is thrown & dragged in the stirrup but not hurt thank God. A grand football match. Many officers & many ladies in the field which looks gay with its flags. Great excitement about the charades. Lionel recites the Thisbe part of one very prettily. Besides ourselves only Mrs. Cameron & the servants as spectators.

18th. Mr. Lawrence comes to make a portrait of A. for some American gentleman.

19th. Mr. Jowett's four friends come to the Terrace.

21st. Mr. Jowett himself comes. I leave his friends at the Football match & go myself to meet him. He takes the proceedings about himself so meekly & sweetly. He says he thinks that the vote is owing to the decree & if so there is ample compensation.

22nd. Mr. Clark comes.

23rd. He & A. go to look at the football match a little.

25th. Mr. White comes.

28th. We are fourteeen to luncheon. Mr. & Mrs. Worsley, Mr. Edmund Venables, the son of Mr. Robertson of Brighton, Mr. Simcocks, Mr. Jebb, Mr. Allingham among our guests. Mr. Henry Taylor calls, also Mr. Latham.

29th. Mr. Lawrence goes. Mr. Jowett reads me some of his Plato which of course we like very much.

31st. We see Mr. Worsley from time to time and are much interested in him.

April

A. & Mr. Wilson planting primroses these days.

2nd. The Worsleys come to say goodbye.

5th. [From this point the entries in Emily Tennyson's journal for April 1864, recording General Garibaldi's visit to West Wight, have been so badly mutilated with scissors, they are largely incomprehensible. Therefore, we have decided to replace the fragmentary remnants with Hallam Tennyson's account of the Italian freedom fighter's visit, as published in his *Memoir* of Alfred Lord Tennyson (volume II). His words are a direct copy of his mother's journal in its original form]:

'We went to the Seelys of Brooke to pay our respects to Garibaldi. A most striking figure in his picturesque white poncho lined with red, his embroidered red shirt and coloured tie over it. His face very noble, powerful, and sweet, his forehead high and square. Altogether he looked one of the great men of our Elizabethan age. His manner was simple and kind.

'A. and I went out to fix a spot in our garden where the Wellingtonia should be planted by him (given to A. by the Duchess of Sutherland, and raised by her from a cone that had been shot from a tree three hundred feet high in California). Poor Philip Worsley's poems had just arrived – the thought of him dying of consumption in the lodging near the bay, mingled strangely with the feeling of this moment and the sounds of welcome as Garibaldi passed thro' the village to Farringford. People on foot and on horseback and in carriages had waited at our gate two hours for him. Some rushed forward to shake hands with him. He stood up and bowed. A. and I and the boys were in the portico awaiting his arrival. On entering the house Garibaldi admired the primroses with which the rooms were decked, and liked the view of our park, and said to A., "I wish I had your trees in Caprera". A. and he went up to A.'s study together, and they talked on politics, A. advising the General not to talk politics in England.

'He told A. that he "could never doubt his country – that he loved her." "*She* never alters!" he said. "Next to God I never cease to have faith in *her*". We introduced Garibaldi to Sir Henry Taylor and to other friends. It was pleasant to see how his face lighted up when he recognized his old acquaintance Mrs. Franklin (wife of Colonel Franklin stationed here): and he greeted the Colonel warmly too. Mrs. Cameron wanted to photograph Garibaldi, and dropped down on her knees before him, and held up her black hands, covered with chemicals. He evidently thought that she was a beggar until we had explained who she was.

'Then we went to plant the Wellingtonia. A. had the large screen put up to protect Garibaldi from the cold east wind. Several strangers were there, and when the tree was planted they gave a shout. On going away Garibaldi shook hands with all and kissed the boys. A. was charmed with his simplicity, but thought that in worldly matters he seemed to have the "divine stupidity of a hero". A. also saw Mazzini, and was struck with his keen intellectual face, and quoted with approval what he had said, "Nothing in this world is so contemptible as a literary coterie".'

. . .

[In the remnants of Emily Tennyson's journal for April 1864, recording the Italian's visit, are the following passages]:

> He [Garibaldi] stroked Hallam's head. We all talked together a little, then Mrs. Seely fetched the boys, myself, & Mr. Wilson away & A. was left alone with him. After dinner Hallam read Garibaldi's Life . . . & A. came in to listen. A very touching life.
>
> . . .
>
> A. dines at Brook and Mr. Seely persuades him to stay all night.
>
> . . .

Mr. Wilson and the boys gather primroses and we put them in in the hall and all the rooms. While we are busy Mr. Humbert calls. I am very glad to see him and make him known to A. and to hear of Mr. Gardiner. Pleasant memories of my Hale House days come with him . . .

. . .

I had committed Pietro to the care of the Housekeeper's room for refreshment, but soon noone could make him understand for he could not speak a word of English. Finally I sent him out with Acott for a walk, and though one talked English and the other Italian, he seemed well pleased and at the end said 'Zoo Zoo!' which was supposed to mean 'thank you, Miss!' I sat with the Franklins until Mr. Seely arrived, as they kindly did not wish to disturb the two, so I sent the boys up with coffee and cake and oranges and raisins, and when Mr. Seely came we all went up.

. . .

[Garibaldi] shook hands with all and kissed the boys. We went with him to the door and bowed and waved. The boys followed him to the Bay where flags were flying. Hallam raised an Hurrah and the people followed him. He ran after the carriage almost to Afton. Garibaldi got up and waved to him. Our friends soon went after his departure, and so ended the memorable afternoon*.

---

*Tennyson commemorated Garibaldi's visit in the poem 'To Gifford Palgrave' in which he mentions the Wellingtonia tree planted by Garibaldi in 1864 opposite the front door of Farringford:

' . . . Or watch the waving pine which here
The warrior of Caprera set,
A name that earth will not forget
Till earth has roll'd her latest year . . .'

Henry Taylor, who was also at Farringford during Garibaldi's visit, wrote the following lines:

'On the Visit of Garibaldi to Farringford'

And there was he, that gentle hero, who,
  By virtue and the strength of his right arm,
Dethroned an unjust king, and then withdrew
  To tend his farm.

To whom came forth a mighty man of song,
  Whose deep-mouth'd music rolls thro' all the land,
Voices of many rivers, rich and strong,
  Or sweet and grand.

Mr. Henry Taylor & Ida & Tina here. We see Mrs. Taylor occasionally. Mr. Allingham here.

14th. Mayall photographs A. & the boys. They take me out in the little carriage day by day on every possible day. Sometimes I ride on the pony, they walking. The Rhododendrons where the big Elm stood splendid, rose red & crimson Anemones in the kitchen garden make it very brilliant. A branch broken from the Garibaldi Wellingtonia & carried away.

19th. We hear that Garibaldi is overdone & returns to Cos & next day we receive from him a copy of Ugo Foscolo's *Poesie*. A. takes me to see the Marsh Marigolds gorgeous in the withy. We have pleasant talks with Mrs. Taylor. She is delighted with the kitchen garden now bright with flowers & well cultivated, the only garden she has seen which reminds her of her Father's at Mount Trenchard he says. A letter of thanks from Garibaldi. We all wrote to him.

23rd. A. & the boys & Mr. Wilson take me up the down. We see the drilling in Easton Field & then go to the upper corner of it & lie by the sea. The first time I have been there since it was ours. Afterwards they take me to the beacon. There is no keeping of Shakespeare's day unless remembering him thankfully is to keep it. A. & the boys take me into the fields or the garden & stay with me under a hedge. A. reads me one day a story from Henry Taylor's note-book which he has been so good as to lend him. He calls & talks about A.'s 'Aylmer's Field' which [he] likes much. The Bradleys come. We go to the Pritchards & see their beautiful greenhouse & hot house & the gentlemen go to the Observatory. I do not like to give Mrs. Pritchard the trouble of taking me.

The boys ride or climb trees or bathe & one day A. plays croquet with them & Ida & Tina.

May

The Taylors go & soon after the Bradleys. Hallam makes an appointment with Rogers to show me the beautiful birds & butterflies from Egypt & the interesting things he has brought for us. Our own garden beautiful with blossoms of Fruit trees & flowers, the air of the down delicious, the green of the young leaves lovely among the pines crowned by the Solent. A. & the boys take me to look at all beautiful things & to hear the nightingales. One rainy day when there was not riding or running up, down green slopes or sitting under hedges, A. & the boys fought each other with rolls of newspaper by way of exercise.

9th. Professor Blackie comes. We like the good, kind, mild man. They all go to the Needles together. The Professor sings 'The Genie with Crooked Horn' and approves of our new crimson carpet with its silver stars. He leaves us for Ventnor. Archbishop Trench has sent his sermon on Shakespeare which I have read.

A. reads me Gladstone's speech on the six pound voters – we are afraid.

Mr. Wilson & Hallam have been so good as to give up their ride that they may help A. & our Lionel to take me to the Beacon so we have tea & dinner kept for them that they may go to the Needles. They clean their own horses afterwards. A. fetches me to hear the Nightingale.

Mr. Warburton & Mr. & Mrs. Garden. It is pleasant to see how much the Gardens enjoy the country. The air is delicious, the sunshine (20th) glorious. Mr. Warburton must go. The rest of the party except Lionel & Hardinge, who return when I return, go on to Brook where A. & Hallam & Mr. Garden splash in the water & enjoy themselves much. The Franklins dine with us and are very pleasant & so passes Louy's birthday.

A. & the boys go again to splash.

24th. The boys put up flags & we have plum pudding in honour of the Queen & of Charlie & Louy. A. & the boys take me up the down. I walk up the steps that were & they race me home in the little carriage down the green road. A. reads some Shakespeare to me.

28th. Mr. Martin Farquhar Tupper calls, gives me a copy of his works, writes his name & mine in it & says that he knows Aunt Franklin. A. & the boys & Mr. Wilson have archery sometimes in Maiden's Croft & I watch them. I see Lionel riding the white pony on the down & he looks a spirit creature.

June

1st. Edmund comes. He has had to cross in a sailing boat because the steamer has run aground. Mr. Allingham comes. All except myself go with him to Beaulieu & enjoy themselves very much. Hallam wants to stay with me. I will not, of course, hear of it. A.

has insisted on my driving in his absence & Hallam also insists. They walk & take me out. A. reads 'My Last Duchess' & others of Browning's Poems.

Catherine Rawnsley & Margaret arrive. The beautiful Mary does not come. Her lover Captain Percy Chaplin who had met her five weeks ago at his brother's wedding heard when in Paris that she was to be at a certain ball & rushes home to dance with her & does dance with her. A. says he is glad that there are still some people young.

13th. Presents from the boys & ourselves to our three years old bridesmaid Margaret and the Swifts [to whom] A. had taken a fancy as a surprise to ourselves, [and] then walks and drives on the Down & to Alum Bay. A. stays with me. People stand in the drive staring at us & one gentleman actually in the Portico.

We see the old Shepherd fondling his sheep. They lift up their faces in the prettiest way to him. When I said your sheep are very fond of you, Shepherd, he replied, "Two ladies were on the down & they ran up & kissed me & they said they had never seen such a thing in their lives". A. takes him to mean the ladies which makes the old Shepherd shake with laughter. Mr. Valentine Prinsep comes in the evening and tells us of the intended purchase of Riter's little property. A. goes to Town on business. Dreary work when he goes. Mr. Prinsep goes with him. I have my boys to cheer me & Mr. Wilson is very kind. One day they walk to the Needles with the 'Love stories' for which the poor lonely soldiers at the Fort have asked. They say it is so dull there.

25th. To-day A.'s poems are to be all printed. Charlie's Sonnets* come next day. I do not think I ever remember the air so divinely sweet for so long together as this year.

27th. We go to Aubrey near Lymington which my Father has bought in order to be within easy reach of us. We are delighted with it. Lionel has taken possession of Uncle Charlie's sonnets & says that he must read them to me himself. He likes so much reading them to me & reads them so beautifully that I cannot refuse tho' I get but slowly thro' them in consequence. The Upham Barrys have had the

---

*Charles Tennyson Turner (1808-79), Tennyson's elder brother, in 1864, published *A Hundred Sonnets.* Previously with Frederick and Alfred he had published in 1827 *Poems by Two Brothers;* this was followed by fifty sonnets in 1830 (highly praised by S. T. Coleridge). After the *Hundred Sonnets* there were other volumes in 1868 and 1873, and posthumously in 1880, *Collected Sonnets, Old and New.*

Terrace and have been voluble in its praise. Colonel Fisher takes it now. I am very busy getting the back staircase altered and a grand arch made before A. returns.

Mr. Wilson is so kind as to look after our people at Aubrey for me.

July

6th. My A. returns. The boys & I go to meet him. I am very glad that he likes the alterations I have made in the hall. He tells me how eloquent Gladstone was on Monday. The Speaker was so good as to make an exception in A.'s favour & let him in tho' all seats were supposed to be full and the Speaker winked hard at his using opera glass. A privilege Mr. Merivale says 'not allowed to ordinary mortals but an honour we pay the Immortal Bard'. The opposition too had their joke, seeing him sit on their side they said, 'We have the Poet Laureate on our side at all events'. A. says that Gladstone's voice trembled when he began speaking & then when he answered Disraeli the whole tide of oratory flowed forth in invective.

9th. Letters from my dearest Father & Louy with good wishes. A. does not like keeping birthdays so I do not tell him or the boys that it is mine. Very pleasant to have our boys & the little Bradleys & Henry Cameron in the Hayfield. We have had on the whole beautiful weather. A. takes me there and all the hay is got in. At the sheep-shearing the Shepherd tells me that the 'Old Lady' meaning his wife sat by him an hour two days following a compliment to our skill as doctors. Day by day the same happy outings for me.

12th. A. & Mr. Wilson go across to Aubrey with Nanny & Agnes in a rowing boat. A noble view of five stalwart soldiers rowing. A. & Mr. Wilson bring back a splendid Salmon Peel, Nanny's gift. A letter from a Liberian Negro. Very interesting.

Our kitchen garden rich with the breath of lilies & I do not think that in any spot on earth the air could be sweeter & more delicate than at the beacon where they take me. We find Mr. Archibald Peel on our return. He recognizes the little pony carriage he chose for us. Mr. Barrett also here. Colonel & Mrs. Franklin dine with us.

17th. The Simeons, Mr. Parlby & Mrs. Franklin. He alas has gone. Louy Simeon says she must see me alone. She tells me that she is going into a convent. This makes me very sad. I tell her that I cannot part from her thus & I beg Sir John to let her stay all night to which he kindly consents. Next day he fetches her & Mr. Wilson bids us farewell. A sad day. I find poor Lionel kneeling by the sofa in the Study fondling Tiny & weeping.

20th. A., Mr. Peel & the boys go out fishing. They take their luncheon with them and come home very bright. Hallam has caught his first fish. They bring a Rock fish with them, a beautiful creature pale green, gold & a little red. A. takes me into Maiden's Croft. We examine a thistledown, teasel flower, beautiful both & the teasel very fragrant, and we gather a lovely bunch of different grapes in the Wilderness.

25th. The Commissioners come to decide the Eastern field question. Our flags up to show how we may be built out of the view for which we have fought so hard and paid so much but the Commissioners are inexorable. Three volumes of Rawlinson arrive from Mr. Wilson. We hear of that most sad event at Yarmouth yesterday evening. Miss T. F. out in a sailing boat with her brother & her lover drowned. She has floated away & cannot be found. The poor lover dived three times. He was taken up by a schooner nearly dead, the brother has also been taken up. It is supposed that she must have been stunned. We are told that they had this morning received her father's consent to their marriage. The body of the poor girl found by a Southampton bargeman just where she had gone down. The Master of the Barge takes her into the little cove near her father's house, lowers his mast & goes to tell the parents . . .

[Back in London, Alfred takes the boys to St. Pauls and to the Tower, which he thinks 'the most interesting thing in London'. The whole family set off for France. In Paris they are impressed by Versailles and the 'barbarous splendour' of Napoleon's tomb. The chief object of their tour is Carnac, though the Druid stones are 'by no means so prominent a feature as we had expected'. Nevertheless, they inspect many Dolmens and a 'great fallen Menhir broken in three pieces' as well as Mount St. Michel.

Overall, this tour of 'King Arthur's country' is a disappointment; it is symptomatic that at one point 'we saw what our coachman said was the Isle of Avalon but we thought it was probably the Isle Domet'. However, the Bayeux tapestry does give 'the feeling of perfect truthfulness' and Emily's diary entry about the Cathedral at Bayeux reveals her rationale for such exhausting and often unilluminating travel – 'A. is, I hope, glad to have been there'.]

September

9th. A pleasant journey home. We cross by Ryde. The sea rough but green & beautiful. Right glad are we to get home. Everything looks clean inside and beautiful outside. We go all of us to look at the new rooms in the Gould Cottage & to call on Shepherd Paul's wife & A. takes me over the Park. The Camerons, Pollocks, Croziers, Mrs. Franklin, Mr. Isaacson, The Dean of Chichester, Enid Guest, Mrs. Dulane, Mr. Allingham call, also Sir John & Lady Simeon & to our surprise Louy with them. She has not been able to bear the Convent life.

22nd. Aunt Franklin & Sophy Cracroft arrive. They have had to sleep at Lymington. Lady Charlotte Schreiber, Enid & Blanche Guest, & Mrs. Alderson call. We walk about the grounds with Aunt Franklin & in the evening A. reads her 'The Grandmother' which is a great favourite of hers & she of his. He says she is charming, so clever yet so gentle & such a lady.

Next day she & Sophy leave. We cannot go with them to Portsmouth tho' we are all invited by Sir Sherard Osborne to see the 'Royal Sovereign'. Lady Charlotte & Mr. Schreiber come to say goodbye. A. reads 'The Farmer' to them.

The day after Col. & Mrs. Franklin & Mr. & Mrs. Frederick Pollock. Mr. & Mrs. Dulane, Enid & Blanche Guest, Mr. Cameron & Ewen & Mr. Neil in the evening.

Our Charlie & Louy arrive. They have crossed in a boat & walked from the Fort & soldiers bring their luggage. Franklin Lushington & Kate & their children come to-morrow.

The day after Frank lunches with us. Sir John & Lady Simeon & Louy dine. Charles & our Louy much pleased with them & they with the Simeons.

We all go to lunch at Swainston & A. & I like the alterations they have made. We call at the Seelys, & see their orchard house & they give us grapes & a golden pippin rather sacred fruits with me for I have seen the old kind in Berkshire held by my Father as best of apples.

Mayall comes to photograph. Lady Charlotte, Mr. Schreiber, & Constance Guest came to stay with us, & there are walks on the down & then to Brook & Donkey Tandems & more sober drives. Col. & Mrs. Franklin come to say goodbye. We are sorry to part from them.

30th. Day of days to me. My Father comes, but he is very tired. The Schreibers go. Poor Lady Charlotte has not recovered the death of her son Augustus. Constance stays with us.

October

1st. My Father & Charlie Louy & go. It seems like some unreal dream that they have been here. Before they go Mr. Cameron & Sir Henry Taylor call & he carries off my Father to photograph him. Mr. Worsley & his brother have arrived on the place. One feels a great interest in them. Poor Mr. Worsley is so very ill*. Mr. Terret's *The Castle of Vitre,* a very pretty watercolour drawing made by himself comes as a gift to us from him. At Mr. Dulane's earnest entreaty made to A. thro' me he reads 'Guinevere' to them in the evening. Mr. Macmillan & Mr. Allingham & Mr. & Mrs. Prinsep & Mr. Watts who have come to look at their newly purchased fields.

Mr. Lear arrives. A most beautiful day & he is charmed & makes a sketch on the South side. We see the Worsleys from time to time & one day Mr. Philip & the boys pelt each other with chestnuts which looks as if he were better. A. & they all call on the Shepherd who has been. It is very pleasant to see Mr. Lear so well & cheerful. He interests A. & me much by his talk of Crete & other countries & other things. Very busy planning the 'Selections' for the People. Mr. Payne is here.

Among the various walks & drives & games A. has a game at football with the boys in 'Dakyn's Hollow'.

31st. Another game to-day after A. & Frank have looked about a site for the new coach house.

November

Baron Bernhard Von Tauchnitz comes. Pleasant & unpretending.

A. reads to me Allingham's Ballads.

8th. He writes his little dedication for the *Selections.*

11th. Mr. Lipscombe comes & next [day] Mr. Wilson leaves us. He has [been] most kind to all & is most anxious to do everything possible for the boys & we are very sorry to lose him.

Busy days about the *Selections.*

---

*Philip Stanhope Worsley, suffering from consumption, died at Freshwater in 1866.

16th. Mrs. Cameron comes to hear 'The Captain'. We send it to be published.

A. has another game of football with the boys. He goes to Town. Poor Lionel has had a bad fall jumping. I bandage him & sleep in his room. He is very tired going only to Grover's to see the cider made! Five hogsheads we have it seems. Thankful indeed am I when the Doctor says that there is no displacement in the arm. A letter every day from my A.

We go to Aubrey. Delighted to find Father so comfortable & happy in his new home. All in it very pretty. The drawing room lovely. C.R.W. hoists his Flag to welcome us. All most loving in their care, hoping to obey A. I went down to the Cabin. Mr. Pritchard came to me & told me of the work he has in hand making the object glass for his telescope, a work of trade not of art generally.

December

1st. The air delicious & delicate. We meet Mr. Eliot Yorke on our return.

3rd. A. arrives rather hoarse but very cheerful tho' with a bad head-ache.

5th. We go to the belt to see if anything can be done to hide Spencer's hideous house. Afterwards we look at the mound being reared to hide the new stables.

A kind letter from Mrs. Gilchrist asking us to stay with her when we go to see 'The Jumps'. I liked the country so much when living with my father at Hale that I think A. will like it too for a second home.

We go to the belt to see how we can block out the dreadful red houses.

The *Selections* both in its plain & ornamented form came. We much prefer the plain but decide on the other not to disappoint the Publishers who have set their heart on it.

Mr. Bird comes about the railways & is glad to get A.'s vote against them. The Bradleys arrive, Mr. Bradley & A. have a game at football with Arthur Bradley, Mr. Lipscombe, & our boys.

28th. Mr. Jowett comes. The boys rush out as usual with the greatest glee to meet him & as usual the chessboard is brought out at once.

Mr. Jowett says that Hallam is very much improved in chess & plays a real game now. The Worsleys come & Mr. Butler.

A. reads the 'Cinque Maggio' & his translation of 'Achilles over the Trenches'.

Mr. Jowett & A. play at football with the boys & Mr. Lipscombe. Mr. & Mrs. Bradley & Mr. & Mrs. Butler dine with us. Poor Mr. Bradley is very unwell from a chill after his football. The [Wednesday?] of walks & football & chess & poor little Lionel tormented by chessmen spearing his eyes . . .

Epilogue

Change was in the air. The rural paradise that had so attracted Tennyson was now subject to a rash of speculative building and development. As Emily recorded,

> 'We hear . . . that the threatened railway with a terminal at the Bay is to be stopt at Hook Hill or Pound Green. Not welcome to us even then' (16 March 1865).

It was time to find a second retreat, less prey to the marauding 'cockneys' who plagued Tennyson every summer, treating him as a bizarre tourist attraction.

On 23 April 1868, the foundation stone was laid for 'Aldworth', Tennyson's new house in West Sussex. It is no coincidence that, at the same time, Emily's Journal seems to lose inspiration, and reduce itself to a mere list of visitors and foreign travel, dull comings and goings.

Yet this also mirrors a diminution of Tennyson's own poetic gifts. Despite occasional work on the completion of *Idylls of the King* – which itself ends in dissolution and exhaustion – his main creative energies were directed to a series of verse dramas, which were neither dramatic nor markedly poetic.

The Journal continues to illuminate, in passing, such emotional undercurrents.

> 'I go with A. into Maiden's Croft. He talks despondingly of Swinburne's book and of the tone of literature in his set as he does now from time to time forseeing the fiercest battle the world has yet known between good and evil, faith and unfaith' (26 February 1871).

The concluding years of Emily's Journal are characterised by such premonitions; a storm which yields 'a fragment of a Vessel bearing a Danish name and a pair of gentleman's boots', a heron seen to swoop down magnificently into Freshwater Bay but 'afterwards, it was alas in the bird-stuffer's shop'. Just as in that wonderful poem of age 'Tithonus', landscape itself is an image of mortality –

> 'The woods decay, the woods decay and fall,
> The vapours weep their burthen to the ground' –

so Emily records a similar mutability in Nature, beautifully rendered.

'He reads to me every evening, takes me to see the gap made by the two great Elm trees which have been blown down near the Farm Cottage . . . the Yew tree already sending out its dust when he blows across it. He reads me 'The Coming of Arthur' (16 February 1869).

There is, however, an equally symbolic savagery in this sense of the old order passing away; 'the great Poplar on the new lawn has fallen & smashed many things'.

The most poignant example of the old order changing occurs just as the Tennysons are about to set off for Aldworth, the 'terrible blow of Sir John Simeon's death' in March 1870.

'A. goes to Swainston for the funeral. All dreadfully sad & trying & seeming all the sadder that the sun shone and the roses bloomed profusely' (31 May 1870).

The death of Alfred's greatest friend on the Isle of Wight, the instigator of *Maud* and a constant source of good cheer, seems symbolically to draw to a close Tennyson's Farringford years, though he would return there each winter.

Julia Margaret Cameron was also soon to leave Freshwater, to return with her husband to Ceylon. Emily's main attentions, judging from the later years of the Journal, were directed towards her children; there are many entries about the schooling difficulties of Lionel and Hallam, as well as the increasing absences of Alfred, in London or abroad. The magical atmosphere of Farringford in the 1850s, a stage on which strutted for a brief hour the opinion-formers and artists, the intellectuals and statesmen of the age, is never quite recaptured. What is increasingly evident is the continuing love between Alfred and Emily.

'Surely love as one grows older has the tenderness of the eve of parting – the long parting. A. never seemed to me so beautiful and touching and I never had moments of the same sort of happiness. Thank God for ever for this time alone with him and our boys' (31 March 1871).

What is also sadly evident is Emily's own decline; always delicate, she seems to ebb vitality, both in the stylistic decline of her Journal and in her feelings – 'the cold mist seems to suck the life out of one Vampire-like'. There is a sense of growing exhaustion, that this most diligent and self-effacing of hostesses is at last worn down by the constant entertaining at Farringford and Aldworth, by the demands of marriage to such a demanding genius.

'Our friends have most of them gone. It is well that the dinners are now at an end for A. has grown tired of them. Very delightful people

> but one's strength is very much overtaxed by the numbers to be entertained & all the work besides' (4 May 1873).

The journal ends with Emily's collapse in September 1874 – 'I became very ill and could do but little, so my Journal ends here' – though she survived for another twenty years.

. . .

The literary style of these reminiscences was 'improved' by Hallam for his hagiographical two-volume biography of his father; rather like Victorian church restorers he replaced simplicity with ornament, bareness with detail. For example, the Tennysons' arrival at Farringford is described by Emily as follows: 'Next day we went to Farringford and looking from the drawing room window thought "I must have that view" and I said so to him when alone'.

Hallam, in no way an eye witness, as he was two years old at the time, elaborates in an over fussy way, much like the late Victorian taste for home design, heavy on detail.

> Next day as they gazed from the drawing-room window out through the distant wreath of trees towards a sea of Mediterranean blue, with rosy capes beyond, the down on the left rising above the foreground of undulating park, golden-leaved elms and chestnuts, and red-stemmed pines, they agreed that they must, if possible, have that view to live with.

Compare Emily's simplicity of description – and syntax – which is far closer to Tennyson's own vision; 'one dark heron flew over the Solent backed by a daffodil sky'. Conversely, it is such directness and purity of response that is so moving, as is her selfless devotion to a great but troubled genius, a touching love affair that was so fully reciprocated. Like Dorothy Wordsworth, Emily's journal records in prose the raw facts that her husband turned into art, but her own response to, and descriptions of, the natural world is still impressive. In her journal the figures of legend – Gladstone, Garibaldi, Victoria, Tennyson himself – are seen at their most human, fragile and living beings. At its least it possesses the qualities of the best soap opera, tracing the tides of family life. At its height Emily's journal is a mirror, reflecting a great poet's response to his world. Tennyson was perhaps the best poet in the language on friendship, not only the deep grief of *In Memoriam* – friendship withdrawn – but the tender welcome of 'To the Rev. F. D. Maurice':

> Come Maurice, come: the lawn as yet;
> Is hoar with rime, or spongy-wet;
> But when the wreath of March has blossom'd
> Crocus, anemone, violet,

Or later, pay one visit here,
For those are few we hold as dear;
Nor pay but one, but come for many,
Many and many a happy year.

The journal presents a succession of such friendships. It is no wonder that Francis Palgrave, a frequent visitor to Farringford, should dedicate his famous *Golden Treasury* to Tennyson with 'the homage which is your right as Poet, and the gratitude due to a Friend, whose regard I rate at no common value'. It is a mark of the Farringford years that, 'Cockneys' aside, the many distinguished visitors came not out of mere curiosity or fashion, but were prompted by fellow feeling, to meet such a friend.

Once settled like a hermit crab, in the remote paradise of Farringford, Tennyson could give himself to the natural world; his long solitary walks on the High Down – poised between woodland and sea – his meditations in the summer house at Maiden's Croft. In this retreat, hand-built and painted by the poet with totems of dragons and serpents, he was surrounded by landscape, haunted by the sea that, in turn, so haunts the narrator of *Maud:* 'Is that enchanted moan only the swell/of the long waves that roll in yonder bay'. The same poem, the masterpiece that he wrote – and endlessly re-read aloud – at Farringford, draws too on Alfred's keen inspection of the stars, viewed through the clear night-time island sky, and interpreted with the poet's characteristic enraged pessimism.

A sad astrology, the boundless plan
That makes you tyrants in your iron skies,
Innumerable, pitiless, passionless eyes,
Cold fires, yet with power to burn and brand
His nothingness into man.

It was once an accepted fallacy that Tennyson's best work derived from the bleakness of the Lincolnshire coast; that his later poetry declined into southern softness. What is made manifestly clear in Emily's journal is Tennyson's creative immersion in West Wight, a strange landscape where even now no two days are either quite the same, where clouds and reflections of sea present an ever-changing panorama, ever shifting moods. It was surely no accident that Tennyson moved to the island on which Keats – his greatest influence – wrote so much of his best work.

Indeed, the journal shows Tennyson's respect for the past, a past of course symbolised by the antique style of Farringford, and the more properly ancient remains excavated in its grounds as recorded in the journal. The most immediately successful of Tennyson's works written at Farringford, *Enoch Arden,* takes as its narrative a folk-tale as old as the seas have been navigable by man; the frequent references to shipwrecks in the journal stress its continued relevance. And his final masterpiece, *Idylls of the King,* sees ancient legend mediated through the figure whom Emily records calling unexpectedly at Farringford shortly after their arrival, Prince Albert. The whole epic was re-dedicated to his memory.

> . . . And indeed he seems to me
> Scarce other than my own ideal knight . . .
> The shadow of His loss drew like eclipse,
> Darkening the world. We have lost him: he is gone:
> We know him now.

Victoria in turn came to know Tennyson, and similarly respect him, even if she is the eternal absence in Emily's journal, the one expected visitor who never arrived.

Of the manifold variety of guests who did visit Farringford, so meticulously recorded by Emily, all forms and conditions of society were represented, from Prince Albert to poor scholars, Americans and religious dissidents. For a poet supposedly cut off from the world on – at the time – a remote island with poor communications with the mainland, Tennyson was visited by, and held intense discussions with, the leading painters, thinkers and poets of the day. He discoursed on patriotism with Garibaldi and the theory of evolution with Darwin, aesthetics with Millais and poetics with Longfellow; and Sir Arthur Bliss performed Bach. Truly if Mahomet would not go to the mountain, the mountain must come to Mahomet. Almost by accident, and much to the advantage of posterity, two women of genius – amusingly tolerated at the time – were on hand to preserve these events, and this haven of intellect, for future generations.

One of these women, Julia Margaret Cameron, is fully recorded in the journal, pestering and encouraging Tennyson with sublime intransigence, like Lewis Carroll – a more fitful visitor to Farringford – developing the bizarre hobby of taking photographs. Indeed, one of the reasons that the Tennysons' stay at Farringford is now the subject of legend (or, in the case of Cameron's niece, Virginia Woolf's play *Freshwater,* satire) is that it lurks, half-recorded and half-forgotten, on the frontiers of the new technology. Tennyson's noble if unkempt profile glimmers from work by the pioneers of photography – Cameron, John Edwin Mayall, Oscar Rejlander – just as his shaky accents declaiming 'The Charge of the Light Brigade' crackle from one of the earliest recordings for the phonograph. But the second of the women to immortalise Tennyson's stay at Farringford is Emily herself, in a journal that shares the posed informality of Julia Margaret Cameron's photographs, and their insight. And yet, as in life, it is Tennyson himself who must have the last word. His wife – who despite her physical frailty survived him – retreats into the background, an ever-loyal organiser and source of encouragement, left to tend Farringford while the poet journeys abroad or to the far reaches of England, waiting always to welcome home the mainspring of her existence.

It was on one of these journeys home, long after Emily had abandoned her journal, that Tennyson jotted down on an envelope – and wrote out in fair copy in his study at Farringford – 'Crossing the Bar'. That familiar stretch of the Solent, between Lymington and Yarmouth, is turned into a metaphor for crossing into another existence, a looking forward to the poet's own death. Indeed, shortly before his death, Tennyson instructed that 'Crossing the Bar' be placed at the end of all editions of his work. It is, however, also a poem of fulfillment. It is his most profound response to the place which was, for forty years, his home with Emily, a place – as recorded in her journal – of occasional sadness, of frequent merriment and good company, a life that resolved youthful pain and bitter self-doubt into mature acceptance, a hard-won serenity.

For all her frailty, Emily was to survive Alfred – who died at Aldworth in 1892 – by four years, although she was quite lost without him. One of Emily's last recorded utterances was 'I have tried to be a good wife'. As her Journal attests she was this and more, a constant but retiring presence, a quiet observer who recorded the glory of her life spent with Alfred for posterity.

Emily Tennyson was laid to rest at All Saints' Church, Freshwater, by the western bank of the tidal river Yar, on 10 August, 1896.

A Dedication to Tennyson's wife Emily

(Published in 1892)

'JUNE BRACKEN AND HEATHER

TO———'

'There on the top of the down,
The wild heather round me and over me June's high blue,
When I looked at the bracken so bright and the heather so brown,
I thought to myself I would offer this book to you,
This, and my love together,
To you that are seventy-seven,
With a faith as clear as the heights of the June-blue heaven,
And a fancy as summer-new
As the green of the bracken amid the gloom of the heather'.

The Tennysons and the Sellwoods

THE TENNYSONS

Rev. Dr. George Clayton Tennyson, the poet's father (1778-1831) who married Elizabeth Fytche (1781-1865); gave issue to

Frederick Tennyson (1807-1898) who married Maria Giuliotti.

Charles Tennyson Turner (1808-1879) who married Louisa Sellwood.

Alfred Tennyson (1809-1892) who married Emily Sarah Sellwood.

Mary Tennyson (1810-1884) who married Alan Ker.

Emilia Tennyson (1811-1889) was engaged to Arthur Henry Hallam at the time of his death; married Richard Jesse.

Edward Tennyson (1813-1890).

Arthur Tennyson (1814-1899) who married (1) Harriet West and (2) Emma Maynard.

Septimus Tennyson (1815-1866).

Matilda Tennyson (1816-1913).

Cecilia Tennyson (1817-1909) who married Edmund Lushington.

Horatio Tennyson (1819-1899) who married (1) Charlotte Elwes and (2) Catherine West.

Alfred and Emily Tennyson gave issue to Hallam (1852-1928) who married Audrey Boyle and to Lionel Tennyson (1854-1886) who married Eleanor Locker.

THE SELLWOODS

Henry Sellwood, the poet's father-in-law (died 1867) married Sarah Franklin (died 1816), sister of Sir John Franklin, the Arctic explorer, and they gave issue to

Emily (1813-1896) who married Alfred Tennyson (Ally).

Anne Sellwood (Nanny), sister (died 1894) who married Charles Weld.

Louisa Sellwood (Louy), sister (died 1879) who married Charles Tennyson Turner (Charley or Charlie).

Chronology

1850—*In Memoriam AHH* published in June; Tennyson marries Emily Sellwood. June; appointed Poet Laureate, November; Emily begins her journal.

1852—Poet's son, Hallam, born August; *Ode on the Death of the Duke of Wellington* published November.

1853—Tennysons move to Farringford, Isle of Wight, November; house becomes theirs in 1856.

1854—Poet's son Lionel born, March; published *Charge of the Light Brigade,* December. Crimea War; Balaclava and Seige of Sebastopol.

1855—*Maud* published in July. Fall of Sebastopol.

1859—*Idylls of the King* (*Enid, Vivien, Elaine* and *Guinevere*) published in July.

1860—Garibaldi leads his 'Thousand Redshirts' to conquer Sicily and Naples. The Camerons settle at Dimbola, Freshwater Bay.

1861—Twelve Confederate States secede from the Union, leading to American Civil War. Serfs emancipated in Russia. Prince Albert dies.

1862—New Edition of *Idylls of the King* dedicated to the late Prince Albert, January; audience with Queen Victoria at Osborne, Isle of Wight in April. Garibaldi invades Papal States, but is defeated. Slaves in American Civil War are declared free.

1863—Battle of Gettysburg. Kingsley publishes *The Water Babies.* W. M. Thackeray dies 24 December.

1864—Garibaldi visits Farringford, April. *Enoch Arden* published, August. Thackeray's daughters Anne and Minny stay with Camerons.

1865—*Selection from the Works of Alfred Tennyson* published, January. Poet's mother dies in February.

1868—Building of Aldworth, poet's summer residence, begun in April, in West Sussex.

1869—*The Holy Grail and Other Poems* published, December.

1870—Sir John Simeon of Swainston dies.

1872—*Gareth and Lynette* published, October. *Idylls of the King* complete except *Balin and Balan* written in 1874.

1873—Refuses baronetcy in April.

1874—Refuses baronetcy again. The *Idylls* completed. Emily Tennyson stops writing her journal because of illness.

1875—The Camerons sell Dimbola and move to Ceylon.

1878—Marriage of son Lionel to Eleanor Locker in February.

1879—Poet's brother Charles Tennyson Turner dies in April.

1880—*Ballads and Other Poems* published, December.

1883—Accepts offer of barony, December; takes seat in House of Lords 1884.

1884—Hallam Tennyson marries Audrey Boyle in June.

1885—*Tiresias and Other Poems* published, December. *Balin and Balan* published.

1886—Lionel Tennyson dies aged thirty-two in April. *Locksley Hall Sixty Years After,* with *The Promise of May* published in December.

1888—Poet severely ill with rheumatic fever; recovers May 1889.

1889—*Demeter and Other Poems* published in December.

1892—Tennyson's last illness, September; dies at Aldworth on 6 October; *The Death of Oenone, Akbar's Dream, and Other Poems* published posthumously on 28 October.

1896—Emily Tennyson dies on 10 August. Buried in All Saints' Churchyard, Freshwater.

Brief Biographies of Famous Visitors, Neighbours & Friends

Allingham, William (1824-1889) Anglo-Irish poet; Tennyson's close friend.

Argyll, Duke of (1823-1900) poet, scientist, Chancellor of St. Andrews' University.

Atkinson, Rev. Francis H., Freshwater Curate; friend of family.

Barnes, William (1801-1886) Dorset poet, friend of Thomas Hardy.

Beaumont, Mr., neighbour and friend.

Bennett, Sir William Sterndale (1816-1875) in 1856 Professor of Music at Cambridge, also conductor Philharmonic Society.

Benson, E. W. (1829-96) first master Wellington College; later Archbishop of Canterbury.

Blackie, John Stuart (1809-1895) Scottish man of letters, Greek Professor at Edinburgh University.

Bradley, George Granville (1821-1903) headmaster Marlborough and Dean of Westminster.

Brodie, William (1815-1881) sculpted bust of poet 1855.

Brookfield, William Henry (1809-1874) rector and chaplain to Queen.

Bruce, Lady Augusta, née Stanley (1822-1876) Queen's Lady-in-Waiting.

Butler, Henry Montague (1833-1918) Master Trinity College 1886; poet's friend.

Cameron, Charles Hay (1795-1880) Mrs. Cameron's husband; owned coffee plantations in Ceylon; succeeded Lord Macaulay as legal member of the Council of India from 1843-48.

Cameron, Eugene Hay (born February 1840) eldest son of Camerons; Colonel in Royal Artillery; married Caroline Catherine Browne 1862 and had four children.

Cameron, Julia Margaret (1815-1879) pioneer photographer; lived at Dimbola, Freshwater; photographed many distinguished visitors.

Cotton, Tiny, married Capt. Speedy; daughter of Benjamin T. Cotton, M.P.

Dakyns, Henry (1839-1911) poet and classical scholar; Farringford tutor 1861-3.
Dempster, William Richardson (1809-1871) composer and singer.
De Vere, Aubrey (1814-1902) Irish poet, dramatist and close friend of family.
Dobell, Sydney Thompson (1824-1874) poet and critic.
Dodgson, Charles (Lewis Carroll) (1823-1898) mathematician, photographer and author of *Alice* stories and nonsense verse.
Doyle, John (1797-1868) painter and caricaturist.
Doyle, Richard (1824-1883) artist and caricaturist for *Punch*.
Dufferin, Lord, of Ava (1826-1902) Governor-General of India.

Elwes, Charlotte, married to Horatio Tennyson, brother of the poet.
Elwes, Dudley, George Carey (born 1837) brother of Charlotte.
Emma, Queen of the Sandwich Islands.

Feilden, Bonchurch friend of Tennyson, Dickens and the Rev. Jas. White.
Fitzgerald, Edward (1809-1883) translated the *Rubaiyat of Omar Khayyâm* from the Persian.
Franklin, Sir John (1786-1847) Arctic explorer and Emily's maternal uncle.

Gandy, children's nurse.
Garibaldi, Italian freedom fighter; stayed with Seelys, Brook Manor, Spring 1864.
Gatty, Margaret (1809-1873) Emily's friend.
Godley, John Robert (1814-1861), with Edward Gibbon Wakefield, founded Canterbury, New Zealand.
Gordons of Northcourt, Shorwell; related to Swinburne, the poet.
Grant, Sir Alexander (1826-1884) Principal Edinburgh University.

Hallam, Arthur Henry (1811-1833) poet's closest friend, remembered in *In Memoriam*.
Hallam, Henry (1777-1859) historian and father of Arthur Henry Hallam.
Hambrough, Albert, of Steephill Castle, Ventnor.
Hamond, Sir Graham Eden (1779-1862) of Afton Manor, Norton; promoted Admiral.
Hatch, Edwin (1835-1889) theologian and Swinburne's friend.
Hood, Francis Grosvenor (1809-1855) neighbour; a colonel killed at Sebastopol.

Isaacson, Mr., Freshwater rector.

Jebb, Claverhouse (later Sir) (1841-1905) Greek scholar and Fellow of Trinity College, Cambridge.

Jowett, Benjamin (1817-1893) Master of Balliol; visited Farringford annually.

Kingsley, Charles (1819-1875) author, theologian and Christian socialist.

Knowles, Sir James Thomas (1831-1908) editor *Contemporary Review*. Designed Aldworth for the Tennysons; a close friend.

Lear, Edward (1812-1888) artist, traveller and Tennyson's friend.

Lipscombe, tutor at Farringford 1864-65.

Locker, Frederick (1821-1895) Clerk Somerset House and Admiralty. Wrote light verse.

Lushington, Edmund (1811-1893) Tennyson's brother-in-law.

Lushington, Franklin (1832-1901) Lear's friend; brother-in-law of poet's sister.

Lushington, Henry (1812-1855), brother of Edmund and Franklin.

Lushington, Tom (1815-1858) brother of Henry, Edmund and Franklin.

Lushington, Vernon (1832-1912) fourth son of Sir Stephen.

Lyall, Sir Alfred (1835-1911) in Indian Mutiny; wrote biography of Tennyson, 1902.

Mann, Dr. R. J., amateur scientist and astronomer; lived at Bonchurch and in South Africa.

Maurice, Rev. F. D. (1805-1872) Christian socialist; poet's friend.

Mayall, John Edwin (died 1867) photographed Tennysons.

Mazzini, Giuseppe (1805?-72) born Genoa; Italian patriot and revolutionary.

Merwood, Mr. Tennyson's gardener and handyman till 1860.

Millais, John Everett (1829-1896) pre-Raphaelite painter.

Milne, Monckton (1809-1895) first baron Houghton; biographer.

Moxon, Edward (1801-1858) Tennyson's publisher.

Palgrave, Francis Turner (1824-1897) editor the *Golden Treasury*.

Palgrave, William Gifford (1826-1888) brother of F. T. Palgrave.

Patmore, Coventry (1823-1896) poet; Tennyson's friend.

Peels of Bonchurch, a family of statesmen, poets; frequently visited Farringford.

Phipps, Colonel Charles Beaumont (1801-1866) Queen's Equerry.

Prinsep, Henry Thoby (1792-1878) master of Little Holland House, Kensington, meeting place of great Victorians.

Rawnsley, Drummond, son of rector of Halton, near Somersby, Tennyson's birthplace.

Rejlander, Oscar (1813-1875) Swedish photographer.

Rossetti, Dante Gabriel (1828-1882) pre-Raphaelite painter and poet.

Routledge, George (1812-1888) publisher.

Schreiber, Lady Charlotte (1812-1895) formerly Lady Charlotte Guest, distinguished Welsh scholar.

Seely, John Robert, squire of Brook manor house; Garibaldi's host, Spring 1864.

Sellwood, Emily, see *Family Tree.*

Sellwood, Henry, see *Family Tree.*

Seymour, Mr., owned Farringford till 1856 when Tennyson bought it.

Simeon, Sir John (1815-1870) Catholic squire of Swainston; poet's intimate friend.

Simeon, John Stephen Barrington (1850-1909), son of Sir John.

Spedding, James (1808-1881) author and essayist.

Spring-Rice, Stephen (1814-1865) poet's college friend.

Stephen, Leslie (1832-1904) in 1867 married Mrs. Cameron's niece Julia Jackson.

Sumner, Charles (1811-1874) American senator and author.

Swinburne, A. C. (1837-1909) poet, spent youth at Bonchurch.

Tauchnitz. Baron von Christian Bernard (1816-1895) publisher.

Taylor, Henry (1800-1886) colonial officer, poet, man of letters.

Taylor, Tom (1817-1880) dramatist, journalist and editor.

Tennysons, see *Family Tree.*

Thackeray, 'Annee' (1837-1919) daughter of novelist, W. M. Thackeray, friend and neighbour of Tennysons and Camerons.

Thackeray, Harriet (Harriet Stephen) with Anne lived at Freshwater after father's death; neighbour of Camerons and Tennysons.

Trench, Richard Chenevix (1807-1886) Cambridge 'Apostle' and friend of Tennyson, Maurice, Sterling and Kemble.

Tupper, Martin Farquhar (1810-1889) wrote popular *Proverbial Philosophy.*

Tyndall, John (1820-1893) scientist.

Tytler, Mary Fraser, second wife of E. F. Watts, married 1886; Tennyson's neighbour.

Venables, Edmund (1819-1895) curate at Bonchurch; antiquary and precentor, Lincoln.

Ward, Louisa, daughter of Sir John Simeon; married Richard Ward; poet's friend.

Ward, W. G. (1812-1882) Catholic scholar whom Tennyson called the 'most generous of all Ultramontanes'. A neighbour.

Watts, George Frederick (1817-1904) famous artist who portrayed Tennysons and their sons.

Weld, Agnes, Emily's niece.

Weld, Anne (born Sellwood) Emily's sister.

Weld, Charles; his wife Emily, youngest sister Louisa.

Whewell, William (1794-1866) Tennyson's tutor at Cambridge.

White, Rev. James (1803-1862) Bonchurch author, historian and friend of many great Victorian writers and artists.

Wilberforce, Samuel (1805-1873) rector of Brighstone; third son of William Wilberforce.

Woolner, Thomas (1825-1892) sculptor and friend of Tennyson.

Worsley-Holmes, Elizabeth, wife of Sir Henry of Appuldurcombe, Isle of Wight.

Worsley, Philip Stanhope (1835-1866) poet at Freshwater, related to the Gatcombe Worsleys. Died of consumption. His classical Greek translations were highly rated.

Further Reading

Lady Tennyson's Journal, edited by James O. Hoge. University Press of Virginia, 1981.

Tennyson – The Unquiet Heart, a Biography by Robert Bernard Martin. Oxford University Press and Faber and Faber, 1980.

Tennyson A Memoir, in two volumes, by Hallam Lord Tennyson. Macmillan and Co. 1897.

Tennyson and His Friends, edited by Hallam Lord Tennyson. *Ibib.* 1911.

Tennyson, by Stopford A. Brooke. Isbister.

Alfred Tennyson, by Sir Charles Tennyson. Macmillan and Co. 1949.

Tennyson, Poet and Prophet, by Philip Henderson. Routledge & Kegan Paul Ltd. 1978.

The Poems of Tennyson, edited by Christopher Ricks. Longmans, 1959.

Studies in Tennyson, by Henry Van Dyke. Kennikat Press Inc., Port Washington, N.Y. 1966 (Originally published by Chas. Scribner's Sons, 1920.

The Tennysons – Background for Genius, by Sir Charles Tennyson & Hope Dyson. Macmillan, 1974.

Letters of Anne Thackeray Ritchie, selected and edited by her daughter Hester Ritchie. Published by John Murray, 1924.

Materials for a Life of A.T. by Hallam Tennyson.

Julia Margaret Cameron, A Victorian Family Portrait by Brian Hill. Published by Peter Owen, 1973.

Julia Margaret Cameron, Her Life and Photographic work, by Helmut Gernsheim; Introduction by Clive Bell. Published by Fountain Press, 1948.

Editors and Artist

RICHARD J. HUTCHINGS

Author of the following books –

Landfalls of the Romantic Poets (Brodie 1964)

Idylls of Farringford – Alfred Tennyson (Brodie 1965)

Dickens on an Island (Brodie 1970)

King of the Mystics – Robert Browning (Brodie 1973)

Young Algernon Swinburne, with Raymond V. Thurley (Hunnyhill Publications 1978)

Tennyson: Selected Poetry (Brodie Notes/Pan Books 1979)

The King Arthur Illustrated Guide (Truran Publications 1983)

Isle of Wight Literary Haunts (Isle of Wight County Press)

Anthologies –

Island of Poetry (Isle of Wight County Press)

The Wordsworth Poetical Guide of the Lakes (Hunnyhill Publications)

West Country Poems of Wordsworth & Coleridge (Hunnyhill Publications)

DR. BRIAN HINTON

Read English at Magdalen College, Oxford and Birmingham University where he obtained his M.A. and Ph.D.; former President of the Oxford Poetry Society and has been for six years Chairman of the Isle of Wight Poetry Society.

His work has been published in –

Between the Lines, Poetry Wales, Doors, Tears in the Fence, ORE and other literary magazines.

He is currently working on a critical study of Thom Gunn.

Poetry published by the author –

Poems from an Island (1981)

The Old Changing Way (1982)

Sotonians (1984)

Breasting the Tide (1986)

Editorial –

Michael Moorcock, an annotated bibliography (1982)

Facets of an Island (1983)

Island Images (1984)

Julian Bell—the artist

Julian Bell was born in 1952, the son of Quentin Bell, the sculptor and biographer of Virginia Woolf, Julian's great-aunt. He is also descended from Maria Jackson, sister of Julia Margaret Cameron. He read English literature at Oxford University before attending the City and Guilds Art School, London. Since 1974 he has worked as a self-employed artist, executing commissions for portraits, landscapes, murals, inn signs, and exhibiting with one-man shows in Cambridge, Freshwater, in the Cylinder Galley, London and in New York. He is married with three children and lives in the village of Rodmell, near Monks House, his great-aunt's last home in Sussex.